# Migration/ Missionary Imagination

First Fruits Press
*The Academic Open Press of Asbury Theological Seminary*
204 N. Lexington Ave., Wilmore, KY 40390
859-858-2236
first.fruits@asburyseminary.edu
asbury.to/firstfruits

# Working Papers of the American Society of Missiology

# Volume 4

# ———— ASM ————

# Working Papers of American Society of Missiology

## Migration/ Missionary Imagination

Edited by
Robert A. Danielson
William L. Selvidge

First Fruits Press
*The Academic Open Press of Asbury Theological Seminary*
204 N. Lexington Ave., Wilmore, KY 40390
859-858-2236
first.fruits@asburyseminary.edu
asbury.to/firstfruits

*Migration/ Missionary Imagination*
Edited by Robert A. Danielson and William L. Selvidge

First Fruits Press, ©2017
Digital version at http://place.asburyseminary.edu/academicbooks/17/

ISBN: 9781621716709 (print), 9781621716716 (digital), 9781621716723 (kindle)

For all other uses, contact:

First Fruits Press
B.L. Fisher Library
Asbury Theological Seminary
204 N. Lexington Ave.
Wilmore, KY 40390
http://place.asburyseminary.edu/firstfruits

**American Society of Missiology (2017: Wheaton, Illinois)**
  Migration/ Missionary Imagination / American Society of Missiology; edited by Robert A. Danielson, William L. Selvidge. -- Wilmore, Kentucky: First Fruits Press, ©2017.
        xiv, 87 pages : illustrations; 21 cm. – (Working Papers of the American Society of Missiology; Volume IV)
        Includes bibliographical references
        ISBN - 13: 9781621716709 (pbk.)
        1. Missions--Theory--Congresses. 2. Christianity and culture--Congresses. 3. Communication--Religious aspects--Christianity--Congresses. I. Title. II. Danielson, Robert A. (Robert Alden), 1969- III. Selvidge, William L..
BV2000.W674 Vol. 4

Cover design by Jon Ramsay

# Table of Contents

# Introduction

ROBERT DANIELSON

In 2016 the American Society of Missiology addressed a variety of interesting topics besides its main topic of Public Theology. Two areas that called out for special attention at this conference were the ongoing concern with the issue of immigration, and a secondary interest in mission and the arts. No topic is probably more important for the church in this generation than the issue of immigration. The globalized movement of the church across cultural and geographical borders has led to a great many issues as well as innovations in the church and how it does mission. At the same time, springing from a wealth of cultural influences, the church is also beginning to seriously explore how art communicates, often in ways that words alone are incapable of communicating. This field is expected to continue to grow and develop in innovative ways in the future. Through the blend of culture and migration it is equally expected that we will see more creative cross-cultural art forms begin to develop and influence the church and how it views worship.

In the opening article of this volume of the working papers, Dae Sung Kim begins with an analysis of why Korean-American churches seem so focused on overseas missions as a major priority for their ministry. Matthew Blanton explores the topic of immigration as one of the most important social issues of our time, and he argues that the field of missiology is especially well placed to study this movement academically. Dae Sung Kim returns with a second paper presented at the conference, originally written for the Korean language track, which looks at how the Korean-American church has developed a strong evangelistic mentality. In part, as a result of their experience as an immigrant people. Byron Spradlin delves into the discussion of how to develop a theology of art and artistic expression for use in the church and in mission. Mark Lewis picks up both of these themes as he relates the experience of using the art of music is working with migrants and refugees in Denmark. In the final article, Geoff Whiteman explores the topic of resiliency in missionaries. Why do some missionaries survive and grow stronger in the face of adversity and why do others choose to give up and go home? Finding ways to measure and evaluate this critical component can help prevent future missionary burnout.

In this work, we are in the second year of a new endeavor of the American Society of Missiology. During annual meetings, many professionals, practitioners, and students present informative papers in a variety of different areas. Often these papers are works in progress, not quite ready for publication, or are ideas looking for professional feedback. Sometimes these papers are just areas expressing the many side interests of the presenters. In most of these cases, these works will not be published as formal articles in *Missiology* or other academic journals, but they still represent excellent ideas and works in progress that can stimulate the missiological community. To keep these ideas alive and active, the ASM decided to launch a series of volumes entitled "working papers." These papers have been presented at the annual meeting and the authors have polished them based on feedback received at the annual meeting, however these papers have not been peer-reviewed and should still be read in that light. They represent current ongoing academic thinking by current and rising missiologists and are presented here to encourage ongoing academic debate and critical thinking in the field of missiology.

# New Missions in a New Land:

## Korean-American Churches and Overseas Missions

DAE SUNG KIM
AFFILIATE FACULTY, MCCORMICK THEOLOGICAL SEMINARY

DOI: 10.7252/Paper. 000080

My fellow pastor, who has completed his graduate study in missiology a couple of years ago, could not join my flight to this conference from Chicago yesterday. It is because he is in charge of a series of fundraising events at his church this weekend such as a rummage sale, a teenagers' car wash, and luncheon meetings. These events are planned for the church's mission trips to Haiti in the coming summer. This year, three teams are organized for the mission trips, but a group smaller than previous years because the church has skipped a mission trip to a sister church on a reservation in Minnesota this year. His church is a local Korean-American church in a Chicago suburb.

This story is not new for Korean-American Protestants. Korean-American churches have sent and supported missionaries to the overseas fields. "A" church in the Chicago suburbs with 600 in weekly attendances supported 40 missionaries and organizations and sent three of their own missionaries, with a leading role in a Christian-based NGO for poor children in the Third World. "B" church (350 in attendance), which I mentioned above as my fellow pastors church, is sending two missionaries and runs one grade school in Haiti and one seminary in Nepal. Both churches keep an annual fund for foreign missions, mission trips and revivals for overseas missions. Both churches spend a third of their yearly budget for overseas missions. These examples are not different from other Korean-American churches which have their involvement at various levels and in diverse ways for foreign missions. Fairly small churches of 30-40 members also put their efforts into foreign missions, usually cooperating with other churches and mission societies. This phenomenon of missionary effort is not uncommon among Korean-American churches everywhere in the U. S.

This presentation will explore Korean-American Protestant churches and their overseas' missions. The main question of this project is why are Korean-American Protestant churches are so passionate and vibrant for overseas' missions? To seek an answer to this question, my working argument is that **Korean-American Protestants have adopted overseas' missions as their ministry priority in their new land**. The purpose of this project is to explain the historical layers that have developed into today's missionary practices among Korean-American churches. This is my brief overview at a glance.

Korean-American churches consist of small local and ethnic churches. The churches have histories going back 40 years or are mostly younger as the U. S. immigration was open to Asians since 1965 and most members are immigrants who are still in the process of adjustment and settlement. Again the small immigrant churches are so much investing their prayers, hearts, and sources for overseas missions, why?

The first explanation comes with the fact that Koreans brought their missionary mind and practices from the mother land. Korean Protestantism began in the 1880s and the young American missionaries were influential teachers of theology and the practices of early Korean Protestant churches. Most of the missionaries including the first who arrived: Horace G. Underwood, Gerhardt Apenzeller, William Reynolds, and Samuel Moffett, were sons of the American missionary movement of the late 19ᵗʰ century led by D. L. Moody, Arthur T. Pierson, and John Mott. Dae Young Ryu states that a half of early missionaries who helped establish churches and schools in Korea came directly from the Student Volunteer Movement (SVM). Their emphases on the missionary mind and practices through evangelism, church planting, revivalism, and foreign missions were deeply imprinted on to Korean Protestantism, and the young churches accepted that the Great Commission advanced through evangelism and missions was the first purpose of the congregation.

The emphasis on missions has permeated the history of Korean Protestantism. Korean Protestantism rapidly grew in the number of churches and members in a century. Today, about 20% of Koreans have identified themselves as Protestants and Protestantism has become the most influential religion in the country. But in the history of Korea this has always been the experience of the minority. As a minority religion, evangelism and revivalism have been the major instruments the churches can use to compete with Confucianism, Buddhism, and scientific atheism. This experiential history resulted in a strong heritage of evangelical faith and practices so that 95% of Korean Protestant churches prefer to be called "evangelical," although the understandings of evangelicalism are often different for different groups. The evangelical emphasis consequently formed the Korean Church's evangelical faith and practices, such as early morning prayer meetings, Tongsung prayer, the church growth movement, and also missionary zeal in order to send missionaries to foreign lands for evangelism, church planting, education, and medical missions.

The evangelical consensus of the Korean churches developed into a foreign missionary movement. In the nation-wide revivalisms in the eighties, Timothy Lee observes the changes of the Korean Church's catchphrase for evangelism, from "Thirty millions to Christ," which proposed home missions in the Korean peninsula to foreign fields into the world. "Evangelization of the Nation Today to the Evangelization of the world tomorrow," was the main theme of World Evangelization Crusade of Korea in 1980. It paralleled the national pride and economic growth among Koreans as well. In the year 1988, when Koreans hosted the summer Olympic games, Yonggi Cho interpreted national development and church growth, preaching "Therefore Korea, as a nation in the world, as a nation that offers sacrifices at the end of time, must spread Christ throughout the world." Now Korean Protestants are very active in sending and supporting overseas missionaries, appointing over 20,000 (24,747) missionaries in 169 countries according to the Korean World Mission Association in December, 2012.

Missionary zeal and practices of Korean-American Protestants are not new for Koreans. They have their roots in their history in Korea, and continue the work in a new place because they believe that missions are the main work of local churches.

A second explanation is that the Korean-American experience of immigration strengthened their evangelical mind and missionary practices. Although the first wave of immigration began in 1903, today's Korean-American community is mostly the result of post-1965 immigration policies. Protestants were never a majority in Korea, at most only 20% of the whole population. But here in the U. S. 60% of Koreans identify themselves as Protestants. Some factors have influenced this phenomenon. Urban middle class Koreans preferred to immigrate to the U. S. and the portion of Protestants among these immigrants was greater than that of the rural low or high classes. Many immigrants were open to Protestantism as an American religion in the process of settlement and assimilation. Even though they were small and spread out, churches also serve as social and cultural centers and formed extended families, building "little Koreas" as well as being a religious institution. Korean Christians keep their evangelistic zeal and practices through inviting, serving, and educating fellow Korean immigrants. As the immigrants increased, Korean-American churches grew and Korean children increasing identified with Protestantism.

Korean-American Protestants developed their own theologies from their immigration experiences. For those who tried to make their American dream real and struggled with cultural assimilation, social degradation, racial discrimination, and hard work, the Christian faith provided a religious, psychological, and social haven and encouraged them by interpreting their difficulties through a theological framework. Sang Hyun Lee understands immigration as God's spiritual calling to pilgrimage. Through the experiences of marginality by recent immigrants, God has called Koreans to be His people and to live out their pioneering responsibility in this new land. Encountering the fact that the U. S. is losing its Protestant distinctiveness, as Kown, Kim and Stephen Warner argue, Korean Protestants find their missionary role by gathering as a strong faith community, building ethnic churches, and sharing their faith with neighbors.

The missionary roles of Korean American Churches always include overseas missions. According to a study by Chang Kim and Chul Chang, the first organized, intentional, short-term mission team was sent in 1984 from the Global Mission Church (Baptist) in Maryland, and since then there has been a ripple effect with more than 50,000 Korean-Americans who have participated in short-term missions over a decade. Furthermore, Korean-American churches are getting more interested in foreign missions projects. As Protestant institutions, local churches planned and worked out their own programs. As individual Protestants, Korean-Americans can find their involvement in missionary work in various ways. They took advantage of their in-between experiences as Korean immigrants in the U. S. They are familiar with travel and foreign culture, and they can speak at least two languages, Korean and English. These advantages enable them to utilize a Korean missionary network from Korea which focuses on Asian countries and from America which focuses on many Latin American locations. Foreign missions is now a growing movement among Korean-American churches.

How can we interpret the growth of an overseas missionary movement among Korean-American churches? Why do they look towards a distant land rather than work on issues in this country?

At a glance, this missionary movement looks like the American movement in the late 19th century that influenced the establishment of the first Protestant churches in Korea. Both had more of a traditional understanding of evangelism and conversion, regarding other missionary endeavors as auxiliary methods rather than primary goals. The missionary views are interwoven with their home church's revivalism, church growth, and national or ethnic pride. Korean-Americans today and American Protestants in the 19th century share Calvinistic understandings of themselves as a people chosen for missions in their generation, interpreting their spiritual blessing and materialistic success.

However, Korean-American churches are minority churches. Their faith experiences are based on their immigrant and minority communities in the U. S. including the visible and invisible walls they have faced between their churches and other U. S. institutions. Language and communication is the most different obstacle for the churches, even between 1st generation immigrants and their children. The churches enjoy their ethnic clusters on Sunday morning, stepping away from their uneasy daily life as strangers or sometimes second-class citizens. The ministry has been busy taking care only of other Korean immigrants. They are checking the Korean news everyday and are crazy about the national soccer team the World cup. An immigrant church is an ethnic island of comfort, kinship, and faith surrounded by the sea of the U. S. society.

In the eyes of islanders, the outside of the island is water. If the islanders are filled with evangelical zeal, they have to look for their ends of the world. If the islanders want to reach other lands, they have to cross the seas. For the islanders who are Korean-Americans, reaching people of other languages and other cultures is overseas missions even though they are physically living only one block away. It is a question for Korean-Americans of which is easier and more meaningful; to be missionaries to American neighbors who they live with, or to send and support foreign missions where they can travel and cooperate with other Korean missionaries. The major concern here is what we can do for the mission and what the field needs from the missionaries, not how far they live from here. For Korean-Americans, the U. S. has enough churches and mission source. It was very hard for Korean-Americans to reach their community as white churches can. But in foreign lands such as Asia and Latin America, urgent needs are waiting for missions which Korean-Americans can join. Yes, it is farther away but it is easier to cross the social and psychological seas. With the missionary heritage from Korea and the immigrant's experiences in America, it is my point that many Korean-American Protestant churches intentionally or unintentionally have adopted overseas missions as the priority of ministry, while leaving missionary work in American society to individual efforts.

Two historical examples tell a common story with today's Korean-American missionary movement. One is the African-American missionary zeal for the African continent in the 19th century. African-American descendents in America particularly had a strong feeling for the evangelization of Africans. Although they experienced urgent struggles against slavery and the risks of a colonizationist scheme, they came together and organized missions for the African continent. For example, A. W. Hanson in a national convention in 1841 showed spiritual interest and interpreted the meaning of foreign missions to Africa claiming: "the destiny of black Americans was ultimately connected with the regeneration of Africa." They shared the evangelical zeal of American Protestantism's white churches in the 19th century, but their mission priority was African people. They had sense of spiritual responsibility and it was possible to participate in African missions. It would be a long and difficult task to change America into a better Christian nation for black people. But now they could share their faith, sometimes with education and science, and devote their lives for African people more effectively than going to white Americans. Through the experience of slavery and faith, they believed that missions to Africa was their destiny from God. James T. Holly, an African-American leader of Haitian missions, maintained in 1859 that for African descendents to "refuse to make any and every sacrifice to advance the interests and prosperity of that nation is to be a traitor both to God and humanity."

Another historical example is the "women's work for women" missionary movement in American missions. Although women played a significant role in missionary societies and supported the first stage of American missions, many women had to join missions as missionary wives. "Women's work for women" respected significant leading roles for woman missionaries especially in the evangelization and civilization of non-Christian women. For example, Mary Scranton (1832-1909), a missionary from the Northern Methodists, established the first modern girls' school in Korea in the year 1886 and taught Korean girls to be leaders of the Korean church and society. Matie Tate, the first female Southern Presbyterian missionary to Korea in 1893, worked for women's meetings and taught a changing life in baptism. But in the America of their time, female students could hardly learn theology with male students, and it took several more decades to obtain ordained leadership in their churches. But they could be effective leaders in foreign fields. This was also the experience of minorities in missions.

The minority experiences of missionary zeal have sometimes encouraged Christians to be active in overseas missions beyond just reaching out to neighbors and changing themselves. Like African-Americans and the women's missionary movement in the 19th century, today's Korean-American Protestants, a minority church, pursue their vision of mission with the sympathy of a minority people in both religion and resources. It is an example of ethnic and immigrant church's mission to other ethnic churches.

The young Korean pastor is now selling stuff and washing cars to increase funds for summer mission trips. The event is not passing without raising many questions: Can they get enough money? Do they need more events? Can the younger generation continue these missionary efforts? Can the church avoid just repeating traditional evangelism? How can they develop ecumenical and cooperative missions? What missions they can do for American society, and how long will church growth and missions go together? And what contribution can they make in world missionary history? With their Korean evangelical history and their immigrant experiences, Korean-American immigrant churches believe and practice overseas missions as the call of this generation for today.

# BIBLIOGRAPHY

Baeq, Daniel Shinjong, Myunghee Lee, Sokpyo Hong, and Jonathan Ro
    2011 "Mission from Migrant Church to Ethnic Miniorities: A Brief Assessment of the Korean American Church in Mission."*Missiology: An International Review*, Vol. XXXIX, (Jan): 25-37.

Bevans, Stephen B. and Roger P. Schroeder
    2005 *Constants in Context: A Theology of Mission for Today*. Maryknoll, NY: Orbis Books.

Cha, Peter, S. Steve Kang, and Helen Lee
    2005 *Growing Healthy Asian American Church*, eds. Downers Grove, IL: IVP Press.

Kang, S. Steve. and Megan Hackman
    2012 "Toward a Broader Role in Mission: How Korean Americans' Struggle for Identity Can Lead to a Renewed Vision for Mission." *International Bulletin of Missionary Research* 36 (2) (April): 72-76.

Kim, Sharon
    2010 *A Faith of Our Own: Second-Generation Spirituality in Korean American Churches*. New Brunswick, NJ: Rutgers University Press.

Kown, Ho-Youn, Kwang Chung Kim, R. Stephen Warner, eds.
    2001 *Korean Americans and Their Religions: Pilgrims and Missionaries from a Different Shore*. University Park, PA: The Pennsylvania State University Press.

Lee, Sang Hyun and John V. Moore, eds.
    1987 *Korean American Ministry*. Louisville, KY: Presbyterian Church in the U. S. A..

Lee, Timothy
  2010 *Born Again: Evangelicalism in Korea.* Honolulu, HI: University
  of Hawaii.

Murphy G. Larry. ed.
  2000 *Down by the River: Readings in African American Religion.*
  New York: New York University Press.

Noll, Mark
  2009 *The New Shape of World Christianity: How American Experience
  Reflects Global Faith.* Downers Grove, IL: IVP.

Pak, Su Yon, Unzu Lee, Jung Ha Kim, and Myung Ji Cho, eds.
  2005 *Singing the Lord's Song in a New Land: Korean American
  Practices of Faith.* Louisville, KY: Westminster John Knox
  Press, 2005.

Robert, Dana L.
  1977 *American Women in Mission: A Social History of Their Thought
  and Practice.* Macon, GA: Mercer University Press.

Ryu, Dae Young
  2001 *Early American Missionaries in Korea, 1884-1910:
  Understanding Missionaries from Their Middle-Class Background*
  Seoul, Korea: Institute of Korean Church History Studies.

Sweeney, Douglas A.
  2005 The American Evangelical Story: A History of the Movement.
  Grand Rapids, MI: Baker Academics.

Warner, R. Stephen and Judith G. Wittner
  1998 *Gatherings in Diaspora: Religious Communities and the New
  Immigration.* Philadelphia, PA: Temple University.

# The Migrant Mandate:

## Missiology, Immigration, and the Local Church

MATTHEW BLANTON

DOI: 10.7252/Paper. 000081

# ABSTRACT

International immigration continues to grow at an unprecedented rate. While there are 244 million international migrants worldwide, The United States remains the most popular global destination, and now is home to one fifth of the world's migrants. This immigration boom brings unprecedented demographic shifts, cultural tensions, and political and missionary challenges. It could easily be argued that immigration is the social issue of this generation. With immigration in the national spotlight, an increasing number of causes, organizations, and disciplines are considering and studying the issue from their unique and often siloed perspectives. However, according to a recent study, less than 2% of Evangelical Christians, and similar numbers of Christians in other faith traditions, report being influenced on immigration by their local church, scripture, or national Christian leaders. There is a clear negligence in Christian instruction on this issue. This paper argues that as an inherently interdisciplinary and transnational field of study, missiology is uniquely equipped to understand and elucidate the complex issue of immigration. Therefore, missiologists have the responsibility to lead, teach, and equip the local church in the United States to understand immigration in their midst, respond to the holistic needs of immigrants, and to partner with immigrant believers as equal partners in the Kingdom.

# THE AGE OF MASS MIGRATION

Migration has been constant throughout human history—people have always moved in search of food, space, wealth, power, and peace. However, this ancient practice was revolutionized in the mid-17ᵗʰ century by the widespread expansion of the newly-formed Western European states (Cohen 1995: 126). Colonialism prompted waves of multi-directional migration. European soldiers, sailors, and merchants moved within Europe and throughout the world, African slaves were forcibly transplanted to the Americas, and indentured servants were brought to China, East Africa, Fiji, and the Americas. (Castles and Miller 2009: 80-3). An influx of capital poured into Europe from around the world, sparking industrial revolutions and innovations in manufacturing and technology (Castles and Miller 2009: 4). The rise of urbanization and wage labor, coupled with increasingly affordable transportation, led to an unprecedented movement later named "The age of mass migration" (Hatton and Williamson 1998: 3).

During this period (1850-1914), 55 million emigrants left Europe for the New World, with the majority (33 million) settling in the United States (Hatton and Williamson 1998: 7). This was mainly a time of *free migration*, as there were virtually no restrictions on immigration in the United States until the late 1880's. Even after the first regulations were introduced, Europeans and Latin Americans were exempted from the rules until after the "age of mass migration" ended in 1920. (Castles and Miller 2009: 84-5). According to the census from that year, there were 13.9 million foreign-born people living in the country, an all-time high of 13.2 percent of the total population, codifying the myth that America was a "nation of nations" and a "permanently unfinished society" (Portes and Rumbaut 2006: xxiii, Briggs 1984: 77). From this point on, the United States would be considered the "most important of all immigrant countries" (Castles and Miller 2009: 84).

This distinction, however, did not slow the waves of nativism and prejudice. The incredible growth of the 19ᵗʰ century was significantly curtailed by a series of reactionary policies and restrictions enacted in the early 1920's. (Castles and Miller 2009: 85). The immigration system was designed to allow immigrants only from "desirable" nations who were expected to easily assimilate into the United States (mainly Western Europe). Consequently, in 1970, the foreign-born population in the United States had shrunk to 9.6 million, a mere 4.7% of the national population—the lowest percentage in American history (Portes and Rumbaut 2006: xv). The period of "restricted immigration" lasted until the passage of the Immigration Act of 1965 that introduced major shifts in immigration policy (Miller and Miller 1996: 10). The bill abolished the old national origin quota system from the 1890's that had prevented most immigration from Asia and certain parts of Europe. Driven by these legal changes, increasing globalization, and worsening economic conditions in nearby nations, the years following 1970 brought a new wave of immigration, increasing the foreign-born population fourfold from 9.6 million to 37 million in 2006 (Portes and Rumbaut 2006: xvi). Different from any other period, the majority of these "new immigrants" were Hispanic, Caribbean, and Asian (Schrag 2010: 163). The most current figures, based on the 2010 census, estimate that there are 40.4 million immigrants living in the United States, comprising 13% of the population. This is only .2% lower than the all-time high from 1920, and the influx of immigrants is only expected to rise (Pew Hispanic Center 2013: 2).

## "ILLEGAL" IMMIGRATION

Immigration from Latin America grew exponentially in the years following the Immigration Act of 1965. The largest group of the "new immigrants," Latinos comprise 50% of the total immigrant arrivals since 1965, with Mexico as the single largest migrant-sending nation (Passel and Cohn 2011: 10). While in the 1940's only 354,804 Hispanic immigrants entered the United States, that number soared to 3.5 million annually in the 1980's (Miller and Miller 1996: 13). In 2010, there were 50.5 million Latinos in the United States, making up 16% of the total population. This was a 43% growth rate over the decade (from 35.3 million in 2000), accounting for a majority of the nation's overall population growth, including native births (Passel, et al 2011: 1). Many of these immigrants came to the United States without legal papers, forming a rapidly growing group of undocumented workers. As of 2011, there were an estimated 11.2 million undocumented immigrants living in the United States (Passel and Cohn 2011:1).

Ironically, illegal immigration soared after the passage of The Immigration Act of 1965. While eliminating the archaic country quotas, the law established a "single ceiling" on the total number of immigrants allowed into the United States worldwide (Miller and Miller 1996: 21). Under this restriction, "no-preference" visas were no longer available for anyone. Thus, the only migrants allowed legally into the US were family members of U.S. citizens or permanent residents, those possessing specific skills, education, or experience needed by employers, and political refugees. "A massive backlog of potential migrants grew immediately," and the *only* way this excluded group could enter the U.S. was illegally (Miller and Miller 1996: 21). The weaknesses of this immigration policy, coupled with the economic suffering of the nearby Central American economies, led to a "system of increasingly organized illegal immigration" (Schrag 2010:164). Not surprisingly, just five years after the passage of the act, illegal immigration was widely considered "out of control" (Miller and Miller 1996: 22).

## CURRENT INTEREST AND CONCERN

As the historical percentages show, the United States is currently experiencing immigration "growing pains" in truly unprecedented ways. Although the current levels are close to the per capita levels of 1920, the overall number is drastically greater, and immigrants are increasingly moving into small, rural communities for the first time ever. Furthermore, the system of illegal immigration which was all but impossible in the 1920s, has captured the fear and anger of many. More Americans are coming face to face with real immigrants, and they are more concerned about the perceived problems and challenges than ever.

A 2015 Gallup poll revealed that for the first time in 8 years, Americans ranked "immigration" as one of the top four problems facing their nation. Despite the concern, 68% reported that they still believed that immigration was a "good thing" rather than a "bad thing" for the country (Newport 2015: 1-3). However, 39% said that they worried about illegal immigration "a great deal," and only 33% are satisfied with how the government is dealing with the issue (Newport 2015:1). A further "77% of Americans said it was 'extremely' or 'very important' that the government take steps to control U.S. borders in order to halt the flow of illegal immigrants" (Newport 2015: 2). As the researcher concluded, "there is a clear distinction between the issue of illegal immigration and those coming across the nation's borders without permission, and legal immigration, which continues to be viewed positively" (Newport 2015: 3).

# ACADEMIC INTEREST

In addition to "average Americans," this growing interest in immigration is also influencing the zeitgeist of academic research. Since the beginning of the "age of mass migration," scholars within the social sciences have focused their attention on immigration. There are generally two sets of questions that surround this phenomenon. Demographers and economists consider the first: "Why does migration occur and how is it sustained over time?" (Heisler 2000: 77). Sociologists and anthropologists focus on the second: "What happens to the migrants in the receiving societies and what are the economic, social, and political consequences of their presence? (Heisler 2000: 77). However, Brettell and Hollifield, the editors of *Migration Theory- Talking Across Disciplines*, contend that in recent times an unprecedented amount of scholars "have turned their attention to the study of this extraordinarily complex phenomenon," resulting in a "volume of research interest in a host of (new) academic fields" (2000: 1). Criminology, clinical therapy, law, medicine, gender studies, political science, and even theology are among the disciplines who have finally decided to join the "immigration game."

Despite the recent growth in these and other disciplines, migration theory and research have existed longest in sociology, emerging soon after the development of the discipline in the United States. Through the years, sociology gave birth to often contradictory perspectives like the (now maligned) "assimilation theory," "Americanization theory," Portes and Zhou's concept of "segmented assimilation," the "ethnic enclave model," and multiculturalism. Despite their unique conclusions, all of these models shared the perspectives and presuppositions of their discipline. Sociologists work "almost exclusively in the receiving society," and base their theories around that research (Brettell and Hollifield 2000: 4). When studying a complex phenomenon like migration that involves many contexts, this focus is myopic. Furthermore, without interacting with and learning from the contributions of other disciplines, the subconscious presuppositions of sociology limit its perspective significantly.

# INTERDISCIPLINARIANISM AND THE BIRTH OF TRANSNATIONALISM

This tendency also applies to the other social sciences involved in immigration research. Each discipline approaches the issue squarely within their uniquely specific perspective and interest. As sociologist Douglas Massey and colleagues summarized, "Social scientists do not approach the study of immigration from a shared paradigm, but from a variety of competing theoretical viewpoints fragmented across disciplines, regions, and ideologies" (1994: 700-1).

In 2000, a diverse group of scholars produced *Migration Theory- Talking Across Disciplines* to address this problem. According to the editors, they desired to bring together leaders from various fields because without an interdisciplinary approach, "research on the subject tends to be narrow, often inefficient, and characterized by duplication, miscommunication, reinvention, and bickering about fundamentals" (Brettell and Hollifield 2000: 2). As "migration is a *subject that cries out for an interdisciplinary approach*," it is incredibly important that each discipline, which brings "something to the table, theoretically and empirically," work together to create a more "unified field of study" (vii).

Recently, more and more scholars have recognized the myopia and other inherent problems within the main field, and "reality-establisher" of immigration research—sociology. Leading transnational migration theorist Peggy Levitt readily admits that "Sociology has been in the service of the nation-state since its inception" (2007: 130). With a narrowly national focus on immigrant incorporation, sociology traditionally ignored the complexity of this phenomenon by opting instead for studies on "how to make Americans out of newcomers" (Levitt and Jaworsky 2007: 130). Recent discoveries and developments in other fields like anthropology, history, and economics shed light on the immigration process, revealing that it was never as simple or uniform as previous scholars had predicted (Levitt and Jaworsky 2007: 130). This led to the formulation of transnationalism as an interdisciplinary theory by which to understand migration in a globalized world.

In the landmark work *Nations Unbound: Transnational Projects, Post-colonial Predicaments, and Deterritorialized Nation-States*, a diverse group of anthropologists share how they "discovered transnationalism" as they compared similarities in their research (Basch, Schiller, and Szanton Blanc 1994: 7).[1] Studying immigrant groups from around the world, these researchers found that their subjects were increasingly contradicting the dichotomist categories of "immigrants" and "those who stay behind."[2] Rather than severing preexisting ties as assimilation theory contended, these immigrants had households, economic activity, political involvement, and *identities* that spanned across one or more nation-states (Basch, Schiller, and Szanton Blanc 1994: 5). Furthermore, these social and political experiences were not "fragmented" as the existing paradigm would have suggested. Rather, these activities, although spread across national boundaries, constituted a "single field of social relations" (Basch, Schiller, and Szanton Blanc 1994: 6). Lacking proper terminology, Basch employed the terms "transnationalism" and "transnational social field" to describe what she was seeing (1994: 5-6).

Beginning with this removal of the "blinders of methodological nationalism," Levitt and Schiller introduce a "transnational social field perspective on society" (2008). A social field is a "set of multiple interlocking networks of social relationships through which ideas, practices, and resources are unequally exchanged, organized, and transformed" (Levitt and Schiller 2008: 182). These authors recognize that individuals within these fields are influenced, in their daily lives, by "multiple sets of laws and institutions" (2008: 189). Their relationships, activities, and even identities respond to state(s) as well as social/cultural institutions, such as religious groups, that exists within many nations and across borders (Levitt and Schiller 2008: 189). To further explain this perspective, Levitt and Schiller propose a view of society and social membership that distinguishes between "ways of being and ways of belonging" (2008: 187). Ways of being are simply the concrete social relationships and practices that people engage. Ways of belonging are practices

---

1    Basch, Schiller, and Blanc admit that this "discovery" happened independently at the same time as others were coming to the same conclusions. Furthermore, even before the development of the term, scholars had observed the "circulation of populations between home and host society" (1994: 7).

2    Anthropologists were able to overcome the weaknesses of sociology because they did not limit their research to the receiving society. With a dual field approach that focused on both the sending and receiving contexts, anthropologists were the first group to recognize the signs of transnationalism (Brettell and Hollifield 2000: 4).

that "signal or enact an identity which demonstrates a conscious connection to a particular group" (Levitt and Schiller 2008: 189). Transnational migrants forge various combinations of ways of belonging and being to carve out social space in their new contexts (Levitt and Schiller 2008: 189-190).

## GOD NEEDS NO PASSPORT

Peggy Levitt encourages scholars of migration to operate with a "transnational gaze," beginning "with a world that is borderless and boundaryless" and then explore "what kinds of boundaries exist, and why they arise in specific times and places" (2007: 22). Following her own advice, Levitt found herself in an area that had been ignored in the social sciences for a long time— religion. Social scientists in general, and migration theorists specifically, have long overlooked the impact and power of religion. Religion was traditionally grouped together with "culture," and it was assumed that the importance of religion would fade in importance as nations modernized (Levitt and Jaworsky: 140). This *secularization theory* assumed that the whole world would follow the pattern of rapidly-secularizing liberal nations in Western Europe. By the end of the 20th century, most intellectuals "had little doubt that modern man had outgrown God" (Micklethwait and Wooldridge 2009:12). Blinded by their own notions of objectivity, researchers simply projected their "modern" Western values and notions of progress on those whom they studied.

Time has proven this hypothesis an utter failure. Rather than wane in influence, religion has actually surged around the world—religious faith and institutions remain vital to "many, if not most, persons in the modern world" (Hirschman 2008: 392). Although building for years, it took significant time for observers and scholars to overcome their presuppositions and take note of what was happening.[3] For example, in the millennial issue of *The Economist*, the publication printed an obituary for God to symbolize the current trends. Just nine years later,

---

3    "Little of substance has changed. The only thing that has happened is that the political classes in the West are waking up, rather late, to the enduring power of religion" (Micklethwait and Wooldridge 2009: 19-20). One of the reasons for this myopia was that sociologists were mainly focused on Europe and other bastions of secularism, while ignoring the "rest of the world" (Micklethwait and Wooldridge 2009: 19).

two editors of the same magazine published a massive treatise declaring that *God is Back* (2009: 12).

Using China and Russia as chief examples, these authors detail how religion has exploded in growth *and* public importance in even the most unexpected places (Micklethwait and Wooldridge 2009: 1-13). Christianity in particular has seen incredible growth in the last century, chiefly across Asia, Africa, and Latin America. Religiosity is even growing in the secular nations of Europe. In a completely unexpected turn, Pentecostalism is now the fastest growing faith in France (Micklethwait and Wooldridge 2009: 14). Contrary to previous "fact," modernity and progress do not threaten religion. Religion is thriving in most modernizing countries, and is actually utilizing the tools of modernity to spread its own message. As the authors of *God is Back* concluded, "The very things that were supposed to destroy religion—democracy and markets, technology and reason—are combining to make it stronger" (Micklethwait and Wooldridge 2009: 12).

In addition to the continued importance and practice of faith worldwide, religions are also central to the discussion of globalization and transnationalism. As indicated in the title, *God Needs No Passport*, Peggie Levitt argues in this work that "religion is the ultimate boundary crosser" (2007: 12). Religious institutions and faiths are founded on universal claims and have always been worldwide in scope. Most major religions spread rapidly through migration, forming some of the first transnational communities in history (Levitt 2007: 12-13, Leonard 2005: 24). Co-religionists join to form cohesive communities that transcend racial, ethnic, linguistic, and national borders (Poewe 1994: xii). For example, in a study of global Christianity, editor Karla Poewe concluded that the best way to understand this phenomenon was not as a *religion*, but as a *global culture* that spans millennia and is "found in indigenized forms in all parts of the world" (1994: xii).

The inherently *transnational* function of global religions encourages, sustains, and influences the lives of today's migrants. Religion is so central "to the immigration experience" that historian Timothy Smith conceptualizes it as a "theologizing experience" (Smith 1978: 1175, Hagan 2008: 5). These travelers use religious institutions to "engender universal identities" and "live their transnational lives" in foreign and hostile places (Levitt 2003: 848). Religions are especially equipped for this task because they connect immigrants to *their* culture and homelands, but also to fellow believers around the world and throughout history (Levitt 2007: 13). As Levitt concludes, "It is time we put religion front and center in our attempts to understand how identity and belonging are redefined in this increasingly global world (2003: 870).

## MISSIOLOGY: UNIQUELY EQUIPPED

Throughout the previous summary of the developments in academic research and discussion on immigration, I have argued a few key points. The best way to consider the complex issue of immigration is to implement an *interdisciplinary approach*, operate with a *"transnational gaze,"* and seriously consider the forgotten area of *religion*. Considering these three requirements, I would contend that missiology is one of the most uniquely equipped fields of study to understand immigration.

In his article "What is Missiology," Ross Langmead explains that while all theological branches have "conversation partners" in other disciplines, missiology has by far the most (2014: 75). He goes as far as to argue that missiology is not even really a discipline "because it is so intertwined with other disciplines." Rather than a discipline, missiology is "a field of knowledge, unified by its common interest and a community of scholars, drawing readily on a range of disciplines" (Langmead 2014: 76). Although missiology obviously has its own presuppositions and end goals, in its very nature it is "thoroughly and willfully interdisciplinary" (Langmead 2014: 76). Charles Van Engen also explains missiology as both "multidisciplinary and centered" (2011). With Jesus at the center, missiology draws from "many skills and many different bodies of literature" (Van Engen 2011) (see diagram below).

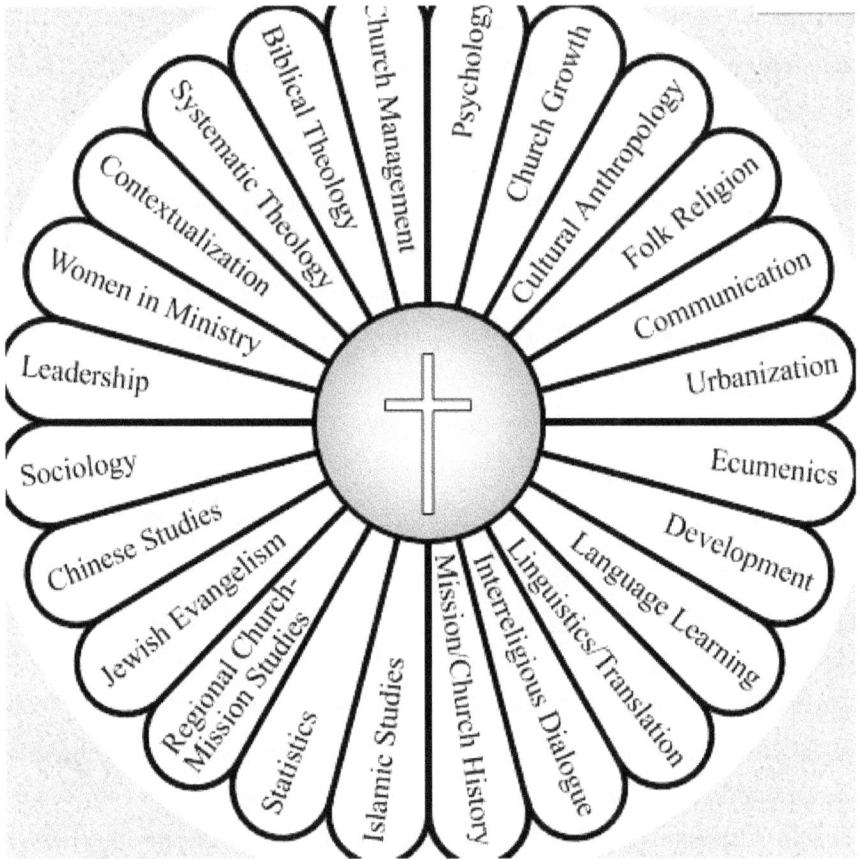

While other disciplines have to intentionally work hard to overcome the limitations of their academic ghettos, missiology inherently exists across a range of disciplines, giving it a unique advantage on the issue of immigration.

According to Levitt and Schiller, the ability to engage the complexities of immigration requires a complete "reformation of the concept of society" (2008: 182). They explain further: "Our analytical lens must necessarily broaden and deepen because migrants are often embedded in multi-layered, multi-sited transnational social fields, encompassing those who move and those who stay behind. As a result, basic assumptions about social institutions such as the family, citizenship, and nation-states need to be revisited" (Levitt and Schiller 2008: 182). Although this has traditionally been a weakness in the discipline of sociology, the inherent worldview of missiology is one committed to a borderless and transnational community of people who despite their differences are united by an ultimate and permanent identity that transcends far beyond nations or even cultures. In other words, while other disciplines might have to work hard to adopt a "transnational gaze," missiology begins with this perspective.

Finally, missiology is uniquely able to understand an essential area of immigration studies that has been so often ignored or misunderstood by other social sciences—religion. Levitt calls for religion to be put "front and center" in this discussion as it is so often a source of identity and meaning for those "in-between spaces," and although that might be a radical call for other academics, missiologists have always included religion and spirituality as an essential part of understanding culture and people. Beyond simply considering religion, missiologists respect and can identify with the religious and supernatural worldviews of those whom they study, unlike so many academics who are blinded by an anti-supernatural bias. For example, both *Global Pentecostalism: The New Face of Christian Social Engagement* and *Divided by Faith: Evangelical Religion and the Problem of Race in America* are lauded works written by Christian authors who are well-respected within "secular" institutions. However, how likely would it have been for secular researchers to yield the same penetrating and emic results? As a research issue, immigration is somewhat unique in the extent that religion plays a central role—giving missiology a unique advantage in the field.

## MISSIOLOGY: UNIQUELY RESPONSIBLE

In his controversial work *Education is Worthless*, Professor Daniel Cottom argues that one of the biggest problems with traditional education is that it "leads us away from practicality" (2003: 2). Although a cliché, the image of an ivory-tower is often true, and as Cottom adds, "we all know that the more educated people are, the more they prefer theory-building, generalization, and creative insight over the transmission of practical skills" (2003: 2). In addition to being interdisciplinary, Langmead contends that missiology is an inherently practical theology, "situation-based" and "shaped by immediate issues, and ideally, (it) shapes our response to those issues" (2014: 75). Missiology does not exist for itself—missiologists are to model and lead the Christian community on how to think critically, strategically, and in a Christian way about how the issues in our world affect the calling and mission of the Church. Missiology should be more about praxiology than orthodoxy—if the discipline is not affecting the beliefs or behavior of the overall community of faith, it is failing.

Given this criteria, how does missiology fare on this issue of immigration? In 2015, LifeWay Research conducted an extensive poll on Evangelicals and their perspectives on immigration. To the question "Which of the following has influenced your thinking most on immigration?," the top three answers were: "immigrants I have interacted with" (17%), "friends and family" (16%), and "the media" (16%). The three *lowest* answers were: "your local church" (5%), "teachers or professors" (1%), and "national Christian leaders" (<1%) (LifeWay Research 2015: 16). Furthermore, only 1 in 5 of those polled said they had ever been encouraged by their church to reach out to immigrants, and only 53% were familiar with what the Bible taught about immigration (LifeWay Research 2015: 17-18). These results mirror a 2010 Pew Religion & Public Life study that found that only 9% of Protestants and 7% of Catholics report that religion is a "major influence" in their views on immigration. The same study found that religiously unaffiliated people are the most likely to express "positive views of immigrants," and white Evangelicals are among those "expressing the least favorable views of immigrants" (Pew Forum on Religion & Public Life 2010).

While missiology is uniquely gifted to study and understand immigration, it is clear that this has not been "trickling down" to the greater Christian community. If the local church, the Bible, or one's faith are not central in a Christian's understanding of a hot-button issue like immigration, something else will fill the void, providing the value-laden lens with which they see the world—be it media, family, personal experiences, or political views. Furthermore, this is not simply about "understanding an issue" from a holistic and Christian perspective—this lack of understanding necessarily influences our behavior toward immigrants—the way we think about them, the way we treat them, and the way that we reach out to them (or don't) in Christian mission, fellowship, or partnership. With unique capabilities comes unique responsibility. It is time for missiologists to escape the ivory-tower and use their knowledge to directly impact the way that the greater Christian community understands and engages the issue of immigration. In the following section, I argue that the most effective way to do this is for missiologists to be active practitioners, teaching, leading, and equipping the local church by engaging actual congregations, facilitating bridge-building, and influencing denominations and networks.

## ENGAGE ACTUAL CONGREGATIONS

From 2013 to 2015, I worked as the Southeast Regional Mobilizer for the Evangelical Immigration Table, a coalition of Evangelical groups advocating for "immigration reform consistent with Biblical principles." Although we had a clear political goal in mind, the overarching goal of our team was to engage local churches and Christians to help them better understand the issue of immigration (both factually and Biblically) and challenge them to respond to immigrants as Jesus would. I spent time in churches all over the Southeast—from college groups to senior citizens, from Presbyterians to Pentecostals, from Georgia to Virginia. It was an amazing opportunity to teach and speak to pastors and *real* Christian people about an incredibly controversial subject.

In virtually all of my encounters, I was met with gratitude by people who wanted to learn more, who were touched by Biblical teaching on immigration, and who had their perspectives completely changed within a few hours. Many expressed frustration that they had believed common misconceptions about the issue that had angered and troubled them—relieved by the truth, they talked about repenting from attitudes of bitterness and seeking out immigrants in their neighborhoods with the love of Jesus. In the range of responses, there was a question that was particularly common: "Why hasn't anyone told me this before?" This is mirrored in the 2015 Lifeway poll where although almost all respondents said they had never heard teaching on immigration, 68% said they would "value hearing a sermon that taught how biblical principles and examples can be applied to immigration" (20).

For academics, it is perhaps more natural to commission polls, do studies, and bemoan the problems of the "local church" from above—it is always easier to criticize than to construct. However, although seemingly obvious, the best way to influence the thinking and behavior of the local church is to spend time with *actual local churches*. Dr. Daniel Carol Rodas of Denver Seminary is an excellent example of this kind of engagement. Although not technically a missiologist, this Old Testament professor spends large amounts of time teaching on immigration to local churches from a decidedly missiological perspective. Passionate about influencing how Christians view the issue, he had done this through his excellent book *Christians at the Border* (appropriate for lay audiences), and he has repeatedly made himself available to speak at churches whenever available, free of charge. I have worked with Dr. Rodas at several events with local churches, and he does an excellent job applying his insight and expertise to the "real world."

# FACILIATE BRIDGE-BUILDING

Although teaching on immigration is an important place to start, presenting this information in a vacuum can potentially lead to well-intentioned stereotyping or patronizing rhetoric and plans to "help" or "save" the immigrants in question. To truly begin to understand the complexities of immigration, majority-culture Christians must humanize immigrants, seeing them as the people and the (oftentimes) brothers and sisters in Christ that they are. With the explosive growth in immigrant congregations nationwide, missiologists have an incredible opportunity to facilitate transformative bridge-building between different congregations and individuals.

In my experience, the most powerful events with local churches were when we brought together mainstream English speaking churches with immigrant congregations. Many people were able to come face-to-face for the first time with the "other," humanizing those who are too often thought of in terms of numbers, figures, problems, or mission "targets." Through worship songs, prayer, and testimonies, many shared how touched they were by seeing their similarities and their common bond in Christ. True bridge-building will go far beyond one-time events and worship gatherings. Ideally, these initial connections will transform into genuine relationships—which is the only setting in which one can truly understand or empathize with the immigrant experience. They also can facilitate Gospel partnerships between groups—which are exciting possibilities and an important step in moving beyond the traditional perspective of viewing immigrant groups as those to be "missionized," rather than those to be agents of mission.

The *Knoxville Internationals Network*[4] is an excellent example of a group that is building bridges and leading local churches in their city on the issue of immigration.

---

4        For more information on KIN and the work they are doing, visit www.kin-connect.org.

Led by Carol Waldo and championed by former missionary Joyce Wyatt, KIN is making amazing strides by engaging *actual congregations* of all types. As often is the case, it is not always "professional missiologists" who pioneer innovative ways of engaging tough issues. By developing relationships with almost every immigrant congregation in the greater region, KIN has hosted "international worship nights" where anyone can come worship together, build relationships, and learn about the cultures in their city. This has led to an amazing movement of Christian unity among these different congregations, and a dedication by many influential churches in the area to teach biblically on immigration, partner with immigrant churches, and work together to serve refugees and advocate for the physical, social, and political needs of the vulnerable immigrant community of Knoxville.

## INFLUENCING DENOMINATIONS AND NETWORKS

For missiology to lead the local church on the issue of immigration, it is essential to be grounded in the practice of engaging actual congregations. However, in order to cover the most ground and influence the most people, missiologists must work at denominational and network levels, influencing, teaching, and equipping leaders who help decide the vision and direction of countless local churches across the nation. Again, this requires "missiological practitioners" with a passion to influence their denominations or networks with their knowledge and expertise.

When I was working with local churches across the South, oftentimes the only reason I would hear back from a pastor or be invited to share in a service was because of the denominational partnerships that the Evangelical Immigration Table had established. For better or worse, local churches are often marked by fierce tribal-like loyalties to their own denominational organs (ex: Wesleyan Church in America) or network allegiances (ex: The Gospel Coalition). In these cases, churches and pastors are wary to accept the teachings or perspectives from an "unaffiliated outsider," especially when it concerns a controversial issue. For this reason, it is incredibly important for missiologists to yield influence within their own spheres of influence, offering teaching and developing tools that will eventually "trickle down" to the congregational level.

For example, Dr. Juan Martinez of Fuller Seminary is very involved in research and teaching on the issue of immigration, but his involvement doesn't end in the academy. Martinez is very active in his own Mennonite denomination, challenging his fellow Mennonites in leadership posts, conference speeches, and denominational publications to "listen to newer Anabaptist voices" in this increasingly "globalized environment." Matthew Soerens, a Church Training Specialist with World Relief and the co-author of *Welcoming the Stranger: Justice, Compassion & Truth in the Immigration Debate* is another excellent example of this network strategy. Working with others at World Relief and the Evangelical Immigration Table, Soerens helped recruit the 11 Evangelical organizations who now form the coalition. He then helped develop practical tools like the "I was a Stranger Challenge: 40 Days of Scripture and Prayer on Immigration," and organized "Preaching Immigration" Sundays. Countless denominations and networks have passed along these resources to their constituents, resulting in high levels of participation and engagement that would otherwise not be possible without the legitimizing effect of the overarching coalition.

# CONCLUSION

Traditionally known as a "nation of immigrants," the United States has continued to live up to its name. With increasing amounts of immigrants from new nations imbedding into more and more unsuspecting places in America's "heartland," immigration will remain a hot-button issue for the foreseeable future. Tapping into this trend, researchers and academics from a broad host of fields continue to address immigration, albeit usually only from within their specific fields and presuppositions. However, recent scholarship contends that in order to best understand the complexities of immigration, researchers must be *interdisciplinary*, working with a *transnational gaze*, and with a special focus on the forgotten area of *religion*. As a field of study, missiology inherently meets these criterion, making it uniquely equipped and able to understand immigration. However, this ability is not reflected among "normal" Christians—a group who shows significant ignorance and problematic thinking on this issue. Therefore, if missiology does indeed strive to be practical and not just theoretical, it is also uniquely responsible for engaging and instructing Christians on immigration, primarily through the means of the local church. This will require practical and active missiologists who are engaging actual congregations, building bridges between believers of different cultures, and strategically working at the denominational and network level in order to have the biggest impact.

# REFERENCES CITED

Basch, Linda G., Nina Glick Schiller, and Cristina Szanton Blanc
    1994   *Nations Unbound: Transnational Projects, Postcolonial Predicaments, and Deterritorialized Nation-States.* London: Gordon and Breach.

Brettell, Caroline, and James Frank Hollifield
    2000   *Migration Theory: Talking Across Disciplines.* New York: Routledge.

Briggs, Vernon M.
    1984   *Immigration policy and the American Labor Force.* Baltimore, MD: Johns Hopkins University Press.

Castles, Stephen, and Mark J. Miller
    2009   *The Age of Migration : International Population Movements in the Modern World.* 4th , Rev. & updat ed. New York: Guilford Press.

Cohen, Robin
    1995   *The Cambridge Survey of World Migration.* Cambridge; New York: Cambridge University Press.

Cottom, Daniel
    2003   *Why Education is Useless.* Philadelphia, PA: University of Pennsylvania Press.

Hagan, Jacqueline Maria
    2008   *Migration Miracle: Faith, Hope, and Meaning on the Undocumented Journey.* Cambridge, MA.: Harvard University Press.

Hatton, T. J., and Jeffrey G. Williamson
    1998   *The Age of Mass Migration: Causes and Economic Impact.* New York: Oxford University Press.

Heisler, Barbara Schmitter
  2000   "The Sociology of Immigration." In *Migration Theory: Talking Across Disciplines*, Eds. Caroline Brettell and James Frank Hollifield. New York: Routledge.

Hirschman, Charles
  2008   "The Role of Religion in the Origins and Adaptation of Immigrant Groups in the United States." In *Rethinking Migration: New Theoretical and Empirical Perspectives*, Eds. Alejandro Portes and Josh DeWind. New York: Berghahn Books.

Langmead, Ross
  2014   "What is Missiology," *Missiology: An International Review* 42 (1): 67-79.

Leonard, Karen Isaksen
  2005   *Immigrant Faiths: Transforming Religious Life in America.* Walnut Creek, CA: AltaMira Press.

Levitt, Peggy
  2003   "You Know, Abraham Was Really the First Immigrant": Religion and Transnational Migration." *International Migration Review* no. 37 (3):847-873.

  2007.   *God Needs No Passport: Immigrants and the Changing American Religious Landscape.* New York: New Press: Distributed by W.W. Norton & Company.

Levitt, Peggy, and B. Nadya Jaworsky
  2007   "Transnational Migration Studies: Past Developments and Future Trends." *Annual Review of Sociology* no. 33 (1):129-156.

Levitt, Peggy, and Glick Schiller
  2008   "Conceptualizing Simultaneity." In *Rethinking Migration: New Theoretical and Empirical Perspectives*, Eds. Alejandro Portes and Josh DeWind. New York: Berghahn Books.

Lifeway Research
    2015 "Evangelical Views on Immigration." Nashville, TN:
        LifeWay Research. http://lifewayresearch.com/wp-content/
        uploads/2015/03/Evangelical-Views-on-Immigration-
        Report.pdf (accessed May 23rd, 2016).

Massey, Douglas S., Joquin Arango, Graeme Hugo, Ali Kovaouci, Adela
Pellegrino, and J. Edward Taylor
    1994 "An Evaluation of International Migration Theory; The
        North American Case," *Population and Development Review*
        20: 700-1.

Micklethwait, John, and Adrian Wooldridge
    2009 *God is Back: How the Global Revival of Faith is Changing the
        World.* New York: Penguin Press.

Miller, E. Willard, and Ruby M. Miller
    1996 *United States Immigration: A Reference Handbook,
        Contemporary World Issues.* Santa Barbara, CA: ABC-CLIO.

Newport, Frank
    2015 "American Public Opinion and Immigration." Washington,
        DC: Gallup, Inc., http://www.gallup.com/opinion/polling-
        matters/184262/american-public-opinion-immigration.
        aspx(accessed May 23rd, 2016).

Passel, Jeffrey S., and D'Vera Cohn
    2011 "Undocumented Immigrant Population: National and State
        Trends, 2010." Washington, DC: Pew Hispanic Center,
        http://www.pewhispanic.org/files/reports/133.pdf (accessed
        May 23rd, 2016).

Pew Forum on Religion & Public Life
    2010 "Few Say Religion Shapes Immigration, Environment
        Views." Washington, DC: Pew Research Center. http://
        www.pewforum.org/2010/09/17/few-say-religion-shapes-
        immigration-environment-views/ (accessed May 23rd, 2016).

Poewe, Karla O.

    1994   *Charismatic Christianity as a Global Culture, Studies in Comparative Religion.* Columbia, S.C.: University of South Carolina Press.

Portes, Alejandro, and Rubâen G. Rumbaut

    2006   *Immigrant America: A Portrait.* 3rd, rev., expanded, and updated. Berkeley, CA: University of California Press.

Schrag, Peter

    2010   *Not Fit for Our Society: Nativism and Immigration.* Berkeley, CA: University of California Press.

Smith, Timothy L.

    1978   "Religion and Ethnicity in America." *American Historical Review* no. 83 (5):1155.

Van Engen, Charles

    2011   "Biblical Theology of Mission. MT500 Syllabus and Class Notes." Pasadena, CA: Fuller Seminary.

# Korean-American Churches and Evangelism:

## An Immigrant Church as Evangelistic Community

DAE SUNG KIM

DOI: 10.7252/Paper. 000082

*Young parents and their children went to a local church. It was their first time attending the church. Although the family's experience of faith and church was almost nothing, their kind neighbors encouraged the family to visit their church and led the family to the Sunday gathering. The family's hesitation to enter the chapel and their reluctant greeting of other members definitely showed that they were first time visitors.*

*What would be the members' response to the visitors at a Korean-American Protestant church? First of all, the welcoming team will greet and lead them to a comfortable pew and keep records of simple information, such as their names, phone numbers, and the ages of the children. Then, a couple of Sunday school teachers would come to hug the little kids and take them to the children's programs. After the Sunday worship service, they will have a chance to meet and talk with the pastor and staff. In the meantime, the welcoming team arranges a lunch table for the visiting family, who can enjoy fellowship time with other members.*

Korean-American churches have emphasized a passion and good practices for evangelism. The word, 'evangelism' has a Greek root; 'εύαγγελιον' which means good news. This suggests that evangelism is to share the good news of Jesus Christ. In practice, evangelism can be defined as a series of processes to introduce the Gospel, invite others to the church community, and empower them to live out the Christian life.[1] Compared to other ethnic churches and their neighboring American churches, Korean-American churches have valued evangelism as their priority for ministry and discipleship. These characteristics of Korean-American churches have resulted in the growth of churches and the evangelization of Korean immigrants through the decades.

What has made Korean-American churches so zealous and give such a priority to evangelism? We can identify one explanation from the customs of Korean Protestant theology. Several Korean Protestant churches emphasize the tradition of the Reformation in faith and life. The theology of "Justification," in which righteousness is achieved apart from sin by believing in Jesus Christ, has become the inception of Protestantism. Through faith and by grace, the reborn soul is saved and the believer continues to practice his faith. This "Regeneration and Sanctification"

---

1        "Evangelism" in *Westminster Dictionary of Theological Terms*, ed. Donald McKim (Louisville, KY: Westminster John Knox Press, 1996), 90, Robert E. Coleman, "Evangelism" in *Evangelical Dictionary of World Missions* ed. A. Scott Moreau (Grand Rapids, MI: Baker Books, 2000), 341-42.

forms the foundation of the Protestant Faith.[2] The "faith" of Protestantism refers to the personal relationship with God, contrasting with the Catholic or Orthodox Church that emphasizes the relationship with the Church. Evangelism is the work of inviting another to this relationship with God and the changed life that subsequently occurs. Traditional Protestant evangelism emphasizes the individual believing in the Gospel and becoming a believer. This forms the basis of a more meaningful and effective way of evangelism, especially in the present day, in which individual faith and decision is more important than those of the nation and family.

Furthermore, Korean Protestantism is closely related to the Evangelical Mission Movement. Many of the foreign missionaries and the first generation Korean leaders that helped establish Protestantism in Korea had their background in an Evangelicalism that stresses rebirth and missions. Among current Korean Christians, the people who are in the religious order that firmly supports Evangelical theology is as high as 95%.[3] The notable feature of Evangelicalism that contrasts with liberalism lies in the emphasis of individual rebirth and Christian mission work. Among several teachings in Christianity, the last part of the Gospel of Matthew, commands that "teaching them to obey" is considered "The Great Commission" and is taken as the first duty for Christians who practice evangelism. Since evangelism leads to social reform and education, the theological flow that puts value in spreading the Gospel and creating Churches formed the mainstream of Korean Protestantism. And the same emphasis that American-Korean churches have on evangelism comes from this very tradition and legacy.

Second, the experience of Korean Christians underlines the evangelizing Christian and the Church. The history of Korean Protestantism starts in the 1880s. Churches formed as foreign missionaries and Korean evangelists started to evangelize one by one, yet Christians remained a minority of the population for a long period of time. The first and foremost mission of the Korean church was evangelism, and participating in this was a responsibility of all Christians. Expressions such as "Christ leads to heaven, disbelief leads to Hell," "Public

---

2       Alister E. McGrath, Reformation Thought: An Introduction, 3rd ed. (Malden, MA: Blackwell Publishers, 1999), 104-110, John Calvin, *Institute of Christian Religion,* Vol. 1, ed. John T. McNeill, trans. Ford L. Battles (Philadelphia, PA: Westminster Press, 1960), lx.

3       Timothy Lee, "Beleaguered Success: Korean Evangelicalism in the Last Decade of the Twentieth Century" in *Christianity in Korea*, eds. Robert E. Buswell Jr. and Timothy S. Lee (Honolulu, HI: University of Hawai'i Press, 2005), 335.

Evangelism," and "Church planting movements" can always be found by exploring the history of each Church. National evangelization and the growth of churches has become synonymous with the reason for our church's existence. Even though over 20% of the Korean population is Protestant only 130 years after the first missionary arrived, the majority of people are still outside of Church. In other words, we have always lived in a land that necessitates evangelism and we have always considered this as an urgent and significant mission. These experiences have been incorporated into the faith and churches of Korean immigrants, who aim to be an evangelizing church.

Third, Korean immigrant churches regard evangelism as their mission in their new land. Immigration enabled Korean-Americans to form their ethnic churches. They had an initial sense of responsibility to evangelize Korean immigrants as their focus group. Extending their understandings of the significance of saving souls and their experiences as an evangelistic community, Korean-American churches have developed their self-identity as a community for evangelizing Koreans in America. They firmly believed that the truth they believed in their mother land is still unchangingly true in this new land, and this truth is to be transferred to their brothers and sisters who are experiencing the harsh reality of their immigrant life. Therefore, the churches' growth through evangelism should be the same mission for Korean-American Christians as it was in Korea.

In its evangelism ministries, Korean-American churches are not different from Korean churches in terms of the content of Gospel and their passion for saving souls, but in their targets, Korean immigrants. Korean-American churches are ethnic havens where Korean in America gather together to worship in Korean. The primary mission for ethnic churches is to form and keep the community so it can share the love of God and the Gospel to their the ethnic group. For Korean-American churches, it was the main goal and the reason for their churches to exist: to invite Korean-Americans and share their faith and mission with them.

In these ways, Korean-American Christians try to embrace the evangelizing mission through their churches' ministries. The faith in evangelism and the experience of immigration has made the mission of Korean-American churches focus on being churches for evangelizing Korean immigrants. This sense of mission brought the growth of local churches and created their characteristic as passionate churches for evangelism.

As Korean-American churches are experiencing the growth of a new generation, however, they are facing serious questions about their form of evangelism. How can a Korean-American church practice their beliefs about evangelism effectively? In what ways can they go beyond the limitation of being ethnic churches? What will happen the their theologies of evangelism as they seek to own future generations?

Korean-American churches have become evangelistic in their faith and practices regardless of their denomination and region. The growing immigrant community, the evangelical tradition, and the social functions of the immigrant society have provided fertile soil for Korean-American churches to bloom their evangelism and church growth. As the surrounding contexts are always fluid, Korean-American churches are recently confronting new changes which challenge their understandings and practices of an evangelism ministry. New changes evidently include the pattern and number of immigrants, post-modern and post-Christendom cultures, theological diversification, and, most importantly, the accumulated experiences of Americanization.[4] Seeking timely responses to these challenges, it is time for Korean-American churches to begin discussions about a new direction in their theology of evangelism while the churches keep their passion and effort for an evangelistic ministry.

---

4      Kwang Chung Kim, SiYoung Park, and Jong Nam Choi, "Demographics and Residential Distribution" in *Koreans in the Windy City: 100 Years of Korean Americans in the Chicago Area*, eds. Hyock Chun, Kwang Chung Kim, and Shin Kim (New Haven, CO: East Rock Institute for the Centennial Publication Committee of Chicago, 2005), 37-39. 37-53. The authors summarize the recent changes of immigration trends from Korea. Helen Lee, "Hospitable Households," 135-37. Craig Van Gelder, "Missional Context: Understanding North American Culture" in *Missional Church: A Vision for the Sending of the Church in North America*, ed. Darrell L. Guder (Grand Rapids: Wm B. Eerdmans Publishing Co., 1998), 35-44. These two discuss post-modernity and the churches of North America. Sang Hyung Lee, "Asian-American Theology: Called to Be Pilgrims" in *Korean American Ministry*, eds. Sang Hyun Lee and John V. Moore (Louisville, KY: Presbyterian Church in the U. S. A., 1987), 39-65. Lee argues that the experiences of Korean immigrants in the U. S. A. construct new perspectives of theologies.

Seeking new directions of the theology in evangelism for Korean-American churches, this study suggests three theological principles. First, evangelism is not just a program or a practice, but a spirituality. In the fields of ministry, it is a deeply engraved misunderstanding that evangelism is doing something, which easily tempts us to follow the successful evangelistic program of churches in Korea or America. When local churches regard evangelism as a way of church growth or instrument for other ministry, it becomes blind to the needs of souls and the mission's spiritual challenges. It is not uncommon that a church's evangelism program holds the market principles of investment, productivity, efficiency and reliance on some effective programs and some members' abilities, and finally the goals and meaning of evangelism become confused.

Evangelism is a spiritual ministry. God initiates it. Fundamentally, it is God's mission to transfer the Gospel and save souls. It is God who gives the mission to God's people. The Holy Spirit is the leader and co-worker with the evangelists. J. Andrew Kirk, a missiologist, defines evangelism as the way and life through which Christians follow Christ. Proclaiming the Gospel, "evangelism", forms the identity of Christians and provides the way to make relationships in the world. Christians are sent for evangelism. Following Jesus is itself a life of evangelism.[5]

Therefore, evangelism is not a project but a process. Evangelism includes whole processes to invite others in to the presence of God as we know and experience it. We need to listen to Elaine Heath's explanation that evangelism is a process to introduce and develop a relationship with God who is speaking, teaching, and healing through the relationship.[6] These understandings enable us not only to do something for evangelism but also to be in the process of becoming an evangelist.

It is my point that evangelism in Korean-American churches should esteem the process of being and becoming an evangelist. Living in God's presence is the way to the Gospel and at the same time to proclaim the Gospel. Evangelism is living to invite neighbors into a relationship with God who they experience through immigration and settlement and evangelism lets them experience the relationship in the same way and in different ways as well. In this process, living with the Holy

---

5    J. Andrew Kirk, *What Is Mission?: Theological Exploration* (Minneapolis, MN: Fortress Press, 2000), 52-55, 60-62.

6    Elaine A. Heath, *The Mystic Way of Evangelism: A Contemplative Vision for Christian Outreach* (Grand Rapids: Baker Academic, 2008), 13.

Spirit is the foundation of evangelism and praying and witnessing with the Spirit in our lives is the ministry of evangelism.

Second, the goal of evangelism is not limited to inviting someone to a conversion experience but inviting them to belong to the Kingdom of God. Traditionally evangelism implies introducing the Gospel to non-Christians in order to make them Christians. Protestant traditions understood that conversion is a moment or a process to confirm a person's level of faith and repentance. They emphasized that it is through conversion, or a process of conversion, that a Christian approaches salvation. The goal of evangelism, however, is bigger and deeper than just conversion. It is an invitation to life in the Kingdom of God. Living as a citizen of the Kingdom of God means salvation of the soul and a life with God, establishing God's freedom, justice, and love.[7]

In this sense, evangelism is intended to invite one not to a local church or specific faith confession, but to a life with Jesus Christ and the hope of God's Kingdom.[8] The definition of evangelism should be extended beyond knowing the Gospel and being baptized to living life as a Christ follower. William J. Abraham argues evangelism is not just for salvation and for a church's ministry, but for the whole relationship with God and his Kingdom in both the temporal and ethereal life.

For example, in Christian mission history there were cases of mass baptism after a short introduction of Christian truth by missionaries. It was true that some missionaries equated counting numbers of the baptized with expanding the Kingdom of God in the colonial Americas and Africa. Today the churches regret these experiences, realizing that evangelism is to lead the listeners to learn the Gospel message, to experience life change through worship and missions, and transform one's individual life and social ethics in the light of the Gospel. Evangelism must include not only the introduction of the Gospel, but also all the teaching needed for the listeners to become Christ-followers and then to be evangelists.

Evangelism that invites anyone to be a citizen of the Kingdom of God consists of the salvation of souls and the salvation of physical, psychological, and social life. In the New Testament, Jesus' evangelism was accompanied by physical

---

7        J. Andrew Kirk, *What Is Mission?*, 29-30.

8        Abraham, Dallas Willard, "Rethinking Evangelism," *Cutting Edge* (Winter, 2001), http://www.dwillard.org/articles/artview.asp?artID=53, accessed by Dec. 31, 2013.

healing and liberation from social evils. The evangelism taught by Jesus proclaims the Gospel, plants churches, cares for the heart-broken, and helps the poor. Serving our neighbors' need and gathering for social justice is also an extended ministry of evangelism. Evangelism is through the word and works of every Christian. We are called to be the light and salt which point to God and God's Kingdom.[9] When Korean-Americans broaden their understanding and practice of evangelism, they can pursue holistic evangelism.

Holistic evangelism which invites people to the Kingdom of God calls Korean-American churches to redirect their identity as an evangelistic church for the Kingdom beyond being churches for an ethnic minority. Overcoming the dualism between soul and culture, proclamation and social justice, and Korean and American, evangelism inspires people to follow the way of Jesus' incarnation. It moves evangelistic priority from the local church or denomination to the Kingdom of God, which is open to all Christians.

Third, evangelism is the mission for which the whole church pulls together. Most Protestant churches in Korea have laid an emphasis on individual efforts, but every Christian is called to witness to the Gospel by word and works. Understanding faith as a personal relationship with God, evangelism is a practice of faith to introduce an individual to a relationship with God. The best resources for evangelism are missions, love, and the proclamation of individual Christians.

In addition to these individual practices, the church should be a community of evangelism. Troubles between church members are a great obstacle for evangelism. Many of the younger generation have been disappointed with the life of church members and left Korean-American congregations.[10] In other words, it is possible that healthier and more biblical churches might attract members from Korean-American churches. Local churches can be attractive to other Christians by praying together, sharing love and cooperating, and doing good works. It requires

---

9        Ronald J. Sider, "Evangelism, Salvation, and Social Justice: Definitions and Interrelationships" in *The Study of Evangelism: Exploring a Missional Practice of the Church*, eds. Paul W. Chilcote and Laceye C. Warner (Grand Rapids: Wm B. Eerdmans Publishing Co., 2008), 200-203.

10      Sharon Kim, *A Faith of Our Own: Second-Generation Spirituality in Korean American Churches* (New Brunswick, NJ: Rutgers University Press, 2010), 54.

that the members of a Christian community do not become exclusive, but reach out and include non-Christians and new Christians.

Reminding themselves to care for neighbors and to remain faithful to the Gospel, a congregation can become a community of evangelism. In *Worship Evangelism*, Sally Morgenthaler points out that holy and spiritual worship works for evangelism by allowing non-Christian participants to experience God, which is its fundamental purpose.[11] It is an agreed analysis that the rapid growth of Korean Catholics these days is the fruit of the church's efforts for social justice in Korea since the 1980s.[12] The effectiveness of the growing Home Church Movement is due to its structure that blurs the division of everyday life and church. Missions to change the church from a members' community to everybody's gathering place represents incarnational evangelism.

For this type of evangelism, an evangelist should be friends with non-Christians rather than a director or a guide. When missionaries evangelize non-Christians in a new field, the listeners pay attention to their sacrificial life and their passion rather than their explanation of truth. In the same manner, remembering that evangelism depends on experience before theory, a good evangelist presents faith by being a good faithful friend and the mission of the church is to form a community of faithful friends.

In this point, Korean-American churches are required to be a community of evangelists, and a community of friends. The tradition to respect relationship has become a double edged sword. It supports the practice of inviting new guests to church while having disharmonized relationships confuses the efforts of evangelism. Evangelism for Korean-American churches is dependent on being a community of faithful friends, which are the local churches.

Korean-American Christians keep their emphasis on evangelism and efforts focused on evangelistic ministry. They continue emphasizing the traditional understanding and practices of evangelism in their new land. The experience of immigration has strengthened their sense of evangelizing missions, especially

---

11    Sally Morgenthaler, "Worship as Evangelism," *REV!* (May/June, 2007), 48-53.

12    J. J. Ziegler, "Where Converts Are Made," *The Catholic World Report* (May 11, 2011), http://www.catholicworldreport.com/Item/679/where_converts_are_made.aspx#.UsNeZ_RDsX8, accessed by Dec. 31, 2013.

while neighboring American churches are losing their passion. Korean-American churches have taken evangelism as the primary mission given by God.

Recent changes in immigration trends and an emerging new generation call Korean-American churches to seek a new understanding of evangelism, overcoming the limitation of ethnic lines. New theological directions pursue broadening the understandings of evangelism as spirituality and holistic process and transforming churches into communities of evangelism. While it takes time and energy, it is an assignment for Korean-American churches, who must continue the evangelism ministry for Korean immigrants and the next generation. The process toward a new theology of evangelism would be valuable addition for contemporary churches in Korea and America.

BIBLIOGRAPHY

Calvin, John
    1960    *Institutes of the Christian Religion*, Vol. 1, ed. John T. McNeill, trans. Ford L. Battles. Philadelphia, PA: Westminster Press.

Coleman, Robert E.
    2000    "Evangelism" in *Evangelical Dictionary of World Mission*. ed. A. Scott Moreau. Grand Rapids, MI: Baker Books.

Gelder, Craig Van
    1998    "Missional Context: Understanding North American Culture." In *Missional Church: A Vision for the Sending of the Church in North America*, ed. Darrell L. Guder, 18-45. Grand Rapids: Wm B. Eerdmans Publishing Co..

Heath, Elaine A.
    2008    *The Mystic Way of Evangelism: A Contemplative Vision for Christian Outreach*. Grand Rapids: Baker Academic.

Kim, Kwang Chung, SiYoung Park, and Jong Nam Choi.
    2005    "Demographics and Residential Distribution." In *Koreans in the Windy City: 100 Years of Korean Americans in the Chicago Area*, eds. Hyock Chun, Kwang Chung Kim, and Shin Kim, 37-53. New Haven, CO: East Rock Institute for the Centennial Publication Committee of Chicago.

Kim, Sharon
    2010    *A Faith of Our Own: Second-Generation Spirituality in Korean American Churches*. New Brunswick, NJ: Rutgers University Press.

Kirk, J. Andrew
    2000    *What Is Mission?: Theological Exploration*. Minneapolis, MN: Fortress Press.

Lee, Helen
    2005   "Hospitable Households: Evangelism." in *Growing Healthy Asian American Church*, eds. Peter Cha, S. Steve Kang, and Helen Lee, 122-44. Downers Grove, IL: IVP Press.

Lee, Sang Hyun
    1987   "Asian-American Theology: Called to Be Pilgrims." In *Korean American Ministry*, eds. Sang Hyun Lee and John V. Moore, 39-65 Louisville, KY: Presbyterian Church in the U. S. A..

Lee, Timothy
    2005   "Beleaguered Success: Korean Evangelicalism in the Last Decade of the Twentieth Century." In *Christianity in Korea*. eds. Robert E. Buswell Jr. and Timothy S. Lee, 330-50. Honolulu, HI: University of Hawai'i Press,.

McGrath, Alister E.
    1999   *Reformation Thought: An Introduction*, 3rd ed. Malden, MA: Blackwell Publishers.

Morgenthaler, Sally
    2007   "Worship as Evangelism." *REV!* (May/June): 48-53.

Sider, Ronald J.
    2008   "Evangelism, Salvation, and Social Justice: Definitions and Interrelationships." In *The Study of Evangelism: Exploring a Missional Practice of the Church*, eds. Paul W. Chilcote and Laceye C. Warner, 185-204. Grand Rapids: Wm B. Eerdmans Publishing Co..

Willard, Dallas Albert
    2001   "Rethinking Evangelism," *Cutting Edge* (Winter). http://www.dwillard.org/articles/artview.asp?artID=53. Accessed by Dec. 31, 2013.

Ziegler, J. J.
    2011   "Where Converts Are Made." *The Catholic World Report* (May 11).,http://www.catholicworldreport.com/Item/679/whereconverts_are_made.aspx#.UsNeZ_RDsX8. Accessed by Dec. 31, 2013.

# Imagination & Artistic Human Expression:

## Toward A Beginning Theology

BYRON SPRADLIN, D. MIN.

DOI: 10.7252/Paper. 000083

To craft a theology of imagination and artistic human expression I believe there are six basic – but foundationally important – theological principles that both church and mission leaders in general, and worship, music, and arts-ministry practitioners more specifically, need to understand. It's necessary to establish these six principles if we are going to responsibly and energetically help church and mission leadership around the world better re-engage and integrate imaginative expression specialists into ministry strategy development and missional ministry practices.

To begin, such a theology must stand on the foundational conviction that worship is central to all of life because God is supreme. But since God is wholly other than his Creation – he, being infinite, non-created, ever-existing, and we being finite creatures with many limitations – God created us with the capacities to engage his mysterious, transcendent reality. He did this by giving us one mind with at least three dynamics of intelligence:

1. Rational intelligence
2. Imaginal intelligence
3. Emotional intelligence

He also created some of us with an unusual capacity for wisdom in imaginative design and expression. Those of us gifted in this way are able to lead individuals and communities into touching the transcendent reality of God himself. As the specialists specifically equipped to lead Christ's Body into the worship of God, it's imperative, then, that we be particularly attuned to the biblical theology that forms the foundation of our specialized assignments in imagination and artistic human expression.

So, with all this said, the six basic biblical-theological issues to consider when forming a foundation for the important place God has designed for artists, musicians, and other creatives to play in the life of the church are:

**FIRST**, we need to establish the biblical definition of imagination and imaginal intelligence. We know from Genesis 1:26, 27 that humans are made in God's image. As such, we possess imaginal intelligence. Dogs, for instance, have instinct; people have imagination. The Hebrew term used here is *yatsar / yester* or "to fashion in the mind before forming something in time and place." This is the term that is often used to describe the work of a potter (e.g., Isaiah 29:16; Jeremiah 18:14). God imagined humankind in his mind, like a potter with a lump of clay, and then actually created us in time and place.

Here we see two capacities: To see what can be before it is and to look through real and observable realities into what is deeper and transcendent. This capacity of imaginal intelligence involves the ability to look at some sort of metaphor or symbol (as we do in any Christian liturgy) and then actually look through these expressions into the underlying reality.

In the Hebrew scriptures the sacrificial system was filled with metaphors, symbols, and expressions – all of which allowed Israel to express their faith in and commitment to the real and living God and his provision and purposes. In the same way today, when we take communion we look through the observable bread and cup and into the deeper reality of Jesus Christ and the giving of his body, the pouring out his blood, the covering over of our sin, and the purging of our guilt.

**SECOND,** we must establish the biblical role of imagination and imaginal human intelligence. It is this role and ability that allows us to engage transcendent reality. Rational intelligence informs us about what is real:

- "This is a bicycle."
- "Here are the pedals."
- "These are the handle bars."

This is valuable information, but you still cannot ride a bicycle until you are fully engaged in the activity. Simply telling someone about a bicycle is not enough to help them ride it. Informing someone of something does not at all mean that a person is engaging in whatever they've been informed about.

The same is true when we approach such transcended realities as . . .

- "God exists."
- "His name is Yahweh."
- "He is Creator of all."
- "Humans rebelled against his rule."

- "Humans experience God's judgment when not rightly related to him."
- "He loves us in spite of us ignoring him."
- "He provides a way to return to him through Jesus."

All these things are absolutely and objectively true, but it isn't enough to just "tell" people about him. Imaginal intelligence allows us to engage with the transcendent realities of these statements. I can tell my wife I love her, but unless I express my feelings imaginatively then I'm simply using hollow words. I need to do things like take her to dinner, bring her flowers, and listen to her. These are the actions that truly represent the words I use. Telling her I love her is not enough. We need to use our imagination to actively engage transcendent reality.

**THIRD,** we need a biblical definition of what an artist is – especially from the standpoint of the Hebrew term for craftsman. There is a family of Hebrew terms for this designation including:

- *Machashabah* (makh-ash-aw-baw') or *machashebeth* (makh-ash-eh'-beth) which means "master craftsman" from Exodus 35:35: "He has filled them with skill to do every sort of work done by an engraver or by a designer or by an embroiderer in blue and purple and scarlet yarns and fine twined linen, or by a weaver—by any sort of workman or skilled designer."

- *Chashab* (khaw-shab') which is rendered "to devise cunningly, to think up, to imagine" (also from Exodus 35:35).

- *Chakam* (khaw-kawm') or "a skilled person" from Exodus 36:2: "And Moses called Bezalel and Oholiab and every craftsman in whose mind the Lord had put skill, everyone whose heart stirred him up to come to do the work."

- *Shiyr* (sheer) or (the original form) *shuwr* (shoor) meaning "singer or musician" as found in 1 Samuel 18:6: "As they were coming home, when David returned from striking down the Philistine, the women came out of all the cities of Israel, singing and dancing, to meet King Saul, with tambourines, with songs of joy, and with musical instruments" (ESV).

Each of these labels are modified by five additional specialized terms:

1. Wisdom, or *chokmah* (khok-maw'), from Exodus 35:31: "... and he has filled him with the Spirit of God, with skill, with intelligence, with knowledge, and with all craftsmanship."

2. Knowledge, or *da`ath* (dah'-ath) (also from Exodus 35:31).

3. Understanding, or *tabuwnah* (taw-boon') and (feminine) *tebuwnah* (teb-oo-naw') or *towbunah* (to-boo-naw') (also from Exodus 35:31).

4. Ability, or *melakah* (mel-aw-kaw') (also from Exodus 35:31).

5. Skillful, or *yatab* (yaw-tab'), from Psalm 33:3: "Sing to him a new song; play skillfully on the strings, with loud shouts."

**FOURTH,** we must understand the biblical role of artists and artistic expression. As we have noted, when you look at how the terms are used in the Hebrew scriptures you see that craftsmen, musicians, and singers are creating environments wherein people touch the transcendent realities of life and, even, God himself.

It is my conviction, then, that the primary role of imaginative expression specialists is to create environments wherein other people enter, and then engage, the transcendent phenomenon of worship. They undertake the work of reverencing and interacting with the transcendent God.

**FIFTH,** we should embrace the biblical purposes of artistic expression, or the arts, in life and in ministry. As I've noted, the purpose of artistic expression is to provide finite humans with the capacity to engage the transcendent. Some examples of this from scripture includes . . .

- God drew Moses to himself via a burning bush.

- God used the Tabernacle as the physical context wherein his transcendent, invisible presence dwelled in the midst of his chosen people.

- God directed his chosen people to express their real-but-non-material faith and trust in him by presenting offerings, observing special days, and engaging in appointed feasts.

- Believers, like Moses, David, Asaph, and the Sons of Korah who expressed their praise to God through prayers set to music and led the community of believers into "song-environments," do the same in worship today.

- Jesus directed his New Covenant followers to repeatedly express gratitude and trust in his saving work through the rituals of "The Lord's Supper" and "Baptism in his name."

- The Apostle Paul instructed believers to regularly meet together for biblical instruction, prayer, and community hymns and spiritual songs.

And, along with the centrality of worship, God has provided artists, musicians, film makers, story tellers, playwrights, novelists, dancers, potters, textile artists, songwriters, singers, directors, producers, sculptors, and many others with the gifts to create environments for the community-at-large to interact with goodness, virtue, beauty, and other transcendent realities. Again, the biblical purposes of artistic expression are to provide finite humans with the capacity to viscerally engage with the transcendent.

**SIXTH**, we must relate imagination and artistic expression to worship. Worshiping the true and living Triune God, at its core, is participating in the mystery of reverentially approaching the morally beautiful, supreme and transcendent God through the work of Christ as energized by his Holy Spirit.

Worship means to bow before God, to honor and acknowledge his supremacy, primacy, and majesty; confessing in awe, wonder, fear, and delight our absolute need of his gracious mercy and provision. Worship is responding with both adoration and action to his self-revealed glory, holiness, love, forgiveness, and purposes through our worship-motivated service on his behalf every day of our lives.

And, since winning worshipers to the true and living God from every tongue, clan, and people is the ultimate agenda he's given us to pursue until he comes again, then those God has gifted with unusual wisdom in imaginative design and expression are absolutely to be front and center in creating contextualized environments and leading others into those environments. In fact, worship will not be effective without musicians and artists working toward those ends because God's Word has revealed this to be the case.

So now, a final encouragement to each of us: we should repeatedly and prayerfully reaffirm before God our request that he deepen each of us in our private and personal worship of God. I am confident that, if we do go deeper as worshipers ourselves, we will have little trouble in seeing our "Theology of Imagination and Artistic Human Expression" align itself with biblical revelation. And, at the same time, we will become a great asset to Church to the carry out the artistic good works of revealing God's truth, beauty, and goodness for which God prepared in advance for us to be "built on the foundation of the apostles and prophets, Christ Jesus himself being the cornerstone" (Ephesians 2:20).

Know this: If we can capture the *Imaginative-Human-Expression-Specialists* of a culture then we can capture the imagination of that culture. We can help them imagine and engage the realities of God's love and salvation and healing, provided through our Lord and savior Christ Jesus.

May God's Spirit give us growing passion for worshiping him. In this way we will fall more deeply in love with the person of Jesus. Then God will pour out through us his creative spirit in ways that will ignite the hearts of church leaders and cause them to fully embrace each artist's vital ministry and role. Then, together, we can far more creatively and effectively "proclaim the excellencies of him who called you out of darkness into his marvelous light" (1 Peter 2:9).

# Promoting Dignity, Community, and Reconciliation Among Refugees Through Diverse Musical Expression

MARK W. LEWIS

DOI: 10.7252/Paper. 000084

## Abstract

This paper will look briefly into the role that music is playing in cross-cultural and missionary encounters with refugees and asylum-seekers. As large-scale calamities continue to force an exponentially increasing percentage of the world's population into displacement and exile, creative expressions, such as music, often are employed to establish connectedness, build friendships, and convey hospitality in ways that are surprising. Though the context for my work and reflection is the North Jutland Peninsula of Denmark, this paper hopefully will provide some insight into how the juxtaposition of applied missiology and music can be fruitful in a variety of cultural settings.

During the past half decade the number of refugees and internally displaced persons in the world has reached levels beyond anything previously recorded in human history. The 2015 World Refugee Survey estimates that 59.5 million people have been uprooted due to war and human rights atrocities, half of which are children. The United Nations High Commissioner for Refugees, António Guterres quoted:"We are witnessing a paradigm change, an unchecked slide into an era in which the scale of global forced displacement as well as the response required is now clearly dwarfing anything we have seen before."[1] Considering the fact that estimates around the turn of the century were around 14 million, the projectile is staggering (Lewis 2004:1).

The primary source of turmoil in recent years can be traced to the outbreak of civil war in Syria, further complicated by the menacing intrusion of ISIS. During this timeframe 11 million Syrians either have been killed or forced to flee, which constitutes roughly half of the pre-war population. The majority of those who have fled have sought refuge in the neighboring countries of Turkey, Lebanon, and Jordan. However, a majority of the headlines in the Western world have focused on the more than 1 million Syrians who have crossed borders into Europe, seeking asylum among Western populations struggling to come to terms with this new reality. Harrowing accounts of boat-crossings across the Mediterranean and Red Seas exacerbate the level of tragedy, as bribes exchange hands and people are herded into precarious vessels built to accommodate only a small fraction of those who set sail for distant destinations such as Greece and Italy. A shocking CNN International news headline on Sunday May 29, 2016 indicates the horrific nature of the situation: "700 + migrants missing or feared dead in Mediterranean shipwrecks."[2]

Yet the crisis in Syria is not the only root cause of massive displacement. In Africa, military conflicts and ensuing humanitarian disasters have blemished the Ivory Coast, DR Congo, and Southern Sudan, and the onslaught of human rights violations in countries such as Eritrea and Somalia have forced many others into exile. In addition to the crises that have plagued parts of the Middle East, Asian countries such as Myanmar, Pakistan, Kyrgyzstan, Burma and Afghanistan; South and Central American countries such as Columbia; and European countries such

---

1       www.unhcr.org, 2015.
2       http://edition.cnn.com/2016/05/29/europe/migrant-deaths/index.html

as Ukraine combine to offer a bleak narrative regarding the current world order. The escalating toll on untold millions of lives has rendered the plight of refugees and the displaced as one of the defining issues of our time.

Throughout Europe and North America, the political repercussions have sometimes been extreme, leading to statements and positions that contradict the Judeo-Christian ethical foundation upon which the West arguably has been built. In light of the rising "backlash" against refugee migration into Europe and beyond, the need for clear missiological reflection and Christian response is critical. There is a compelling theological mandate for demonstrating hospitality to foreigners in need. Jesus clearly states that we are to welcome the stranger (Matthew 25:35), and the message likewise is reflected in several New Testament epistles (cf. Romans 12:13 and 15:7, Hebrews 13:2, and I Peter 4:9, among others). Empathizing with sojourners while remembering Israel's past experiences of exodus and exile is thematic in the Old Testament (cf. Exodus 22:21, Leviticus 19:33 and 24:22, Deuteronomy 10:18, among many others). Even Jesus and his family were refugees in Egypt while fleeing the pogrom of King Herod (Matthew 2:13), thus implying an inherent Christian empathy for oppressed and disenfranchised people around the world.

Governments are understandably required to reflect sensible policies regarding economics and security; however, the larger ethical concerns involve the unleashing of xenophobia targeted against an already traumatized population. When the Danish government, for example, recently enacted a bill allowing for the confiscation of money and other valuables worth more than approximately $2,000, the "good Samaritan" efforts so characteristic of the actions of many Danes became undermined, thus fueling mutual mistrust and animosity.[3] As other countries either close their borders or threaten to do so, the tension caused by the possibility of forced repatriation adds more anxiety to an already unbearable situation. Further marginalization and exclusion caused by residence in a foreign country – each with its own set of rules (written and unwritten), expectations, and moral assumptions – likewise poses a different set of challenges. While the Western media and government spokespersons employ terms such as "refugee crisis," host populations

---

3      See      http://jyllands-posten.dk/politik/ECE8313942/St%C3%B8jberg-efter-nazi-sammenligninger-Kun-rimeligt-at-tage-v%C3%A6rdier-fra-flygtninge, Jyllands Post December 12, 2015.

are enticed to think of it as their own "crisis," precipitated by the deluge of foreigners overrunning their cultural territory. Missiological insights can challenge people to think and respond differently. In such an unstable environment, people from all backgrounds need to be informed about the inevitable tensions that occur when differing cultures and worldviews meet, in addition to related issues of culture shock, psychological trauma, ethnocentrism, and the like. As representatives of the Gospel of grace and compassion, Christians with a developed sensitivity toward multiculturalism and justice are needed in every sphere of society. One can affirm that missiology is uniquely positioned to promote understanding and reconciliation in light of the current crisis, by engendering a theology of hospitality towards "the least of these."

Although the influx of displaced persons in the West can call for a wide variety of missiological responses, an overlooked yet obvious expression centers on the use of music and other artistic expressions. During the many refugee gatherings that take place throughout Denmark – whether in refugee centers, churches, schools, on pedestrian streets, etc. – people often will notice three elements that almost always are present: music, dance, and food! As much as anything else, music provides opportunities for cultural expression, learning, and even emotional catharsis. In my own experience as senior pastor, mission secretary, musician, and local teacher of adult courses in world religions and culture studies, I have had the opportunity to observe how the employment of music during varieties of cross-cultural events is about much more than entertainment. The indigenous music of the differing displaced populations provides a glimpse into the collective "heart" of their culture, and it facilitates opportunities for cultural exchange in ways that discursive communication often cannot match.

## Music as Therapy

Since World War II, awareness of the medicinal value of music in treating victims of stress and depression has developed into a new discipline – music therapy. According to John Powell, it began simply as an attempt to bring comfort to traumatized war veterans, and grew as hospital staff began to realize the positive effects of music on the physical and mental well-being of their patients (Powell 2016:74). As musicians and musicologists became more involved in health care, a plethora of studies have emerged, which document the impact of music on the immune system, pain and even the reduction of symptoms from Parkinson's disease (2016:74-80).[4]

Reflections by musicians working with refugees around the world likewise point to the therapeutic role of music. There is no shortage of published case studies, including work done among traumatized refugees, and a series of documentaries by journalist Alex Petrapoulos provides examples. Recounting life stories in the Zaatari refugee camp outside of Mafraq, Jordan, Petrapoulos summarizes that almost all songs and poems share a common theme: the longing for home (Petrapoulos 2016). In a series of short film clips about displaced Syrians residing in a camp with around 79,000 other residents, Petrapoulos suggests how songs provide a catharsis, thereby assisting in the process of healing from the inexpressible anguish experienced by most residents, as well as establishing a sense of connectedness with home. Most importantly, music helps them to maintain hope. In my own formal and informal conversations with Syrian refugees in Denmark, I have discovered that the desire to return home to a stable and rebuilding Syria is by far the strongest impulse. Since language imposes a formidable barrier (only a very small percentage can communicate adequately in English), music becomes the primary conduit for conveying their deepest emotions.

The nexus between music therapy and refugee outreach has received attention for several decades, as evidenced by a 1998 collection of essays, entitled *Arts Therapist, Refugees and Migrants Reaching Across Borders*. In one particular article, focus was given to treatment of traumatized Vietnamese refugees, many of whom had been diagnosed with serious mental disorders related to torture and violence. In their case, music therapy as "treatment" was employed to provide a median for expressing feelings such as homesickness, loneliness, and despair. Use of indigenous music was especially helpful due to language issues, since music can be used as a form of non-verbal communication. The familiarity of the music for refugee patients was also credited for enabling them to maintain their own cultural identity, creating opportunities for socially constructive interaction, and promoting a means of self-expression (Doktor 1998:82-83).

---

4        The relationship of music and health continues to be explored by medical professionals. An example is provided by a personal friend, Danish neurologist Peter Michael Nielsen, who has been given a sizable grant by the Danish government to fund a project dealing with the impact of tones, especially bass tones, on chronic pain relief and the process of healing.

Doktor, et al. once again remind the reader of the perilous plight of most displaced persons. One should, at any rate, not forget that their past events often are overwhelming. They have lost everything and are forced to rely on the charity of a foreign country. The onslaught of trauma and homelessness take a devastating toll on their emotional state. And fear and uncertainty reduce life to a matter of survival. Under these circumstances, the need to respect and acknowledge emotions such as longing, fear, anger, joy, grief, etc. becomes magnified. A therapeutic approach to music therefore should begin by seeking common ground in terms of feelings and experiences that may be shared collectively. Music (i.e., sound, rhythm, and melody) is uniquely capable of achieving this goal, even among some of the most introverted personalities (1998:84).

A related analysis is provided by Sarah Scroope and Rosemary Signorelli. As music therapists engaged in refugee work, they convey an understanding of the impact that music in general has in evoking expressions of personal emotions, as well as providing a context for celebrating family and community life. Scroope and Signorelli have utilized music to address the needs of refugees affected by war, violence, dispossession, and loss through a combination of listening, playing, writing, recording, movement, and dance (Scroope 2010:36). Their work at the time focused primarily on contact with Iraqi women and children from minority religious communities, who had fled to Australia. By teaching songs to preschoolers and their mothers, it became for them apparent how music can promote literacy and enhance child development (2010:36). Some of the sessions included popular and traditional music from Iraq, where all participants were encouraged to sing along. One of the advantages of music in cross-cultural settings is that it empowers participants by enabling them to use their own voices, thus deepening the sense of shared culture. As their work points out, energetic singing has physiological benefits by releasing endorphins, which in turn can reduce feelings of stress, anxiety, and depression (2010:36).

However, there are a couple of caveats to the use of music in therapeutic contexts. In one particular case, for example, music conjured traumatic memories in a boy from Sierra Leone, who witnessed the murder of his father to the sound of drumming (Doktor 1998:89). Since verbal communication is often exceedingly difficult, at least without the help of translators, it is difficult for practitioners to understand whether or not meaning constructions have become distorted due to unspeakable circumstances. It is therefore incumbent upon those who employ music as therapy to be sensitive to the diversity of meanings, as well as the array of emotional and cognitive factors that may be present during such gatherings. In our own contact with large groups of refugees, we are challenged to remember that groups consist of individuals, who embody their own life experiences, thought processes, emotional makeup, and personality. In other words, it is important in our work to see each person as uniquely created in God's image.

Nevertheless, as Scroope and Signorelli point out, contact with refugee children through musical exchange can reap many benefits. This is something to which a group from my own context enthusiastically can attest. In January 2016 members of an outreach committee from my local Methodist church acted on a suggestion that emerged in conversation with volunteer coordinators at a nearby refugee center. It involved initiating a bi-weekly playschool for pre-schoolers and their mothers, to be held at the center. The program quickly gained a good reputation, and has since served as a template for the establishment of similar programs in other centers. As one might imagine, music is a key component, with special emphasis on teaching basic Danish children's songs that involve gestures and movement.[5] As the primary leader sings songs about colors, animals, balloons, and other subjects with the aid of props (and occasional guitar accompaniment by her missiologist/pastor!), mothers often join in with their children. The success of the program relates in part to the nurturing of cognitive development in children; however, it has gained broad appeal, most likely because it provides an activity that breaks the monotony of life "on hold" in a refugee camp, while presenting a relaxed introduction to certain facets of Danish life and culture. In this way, such activities play a small role in helping to ameliorate the otherwise difficult process of integration into a foreign culture.

## Music, Community, and Emotions

Quite often, people groups are encouraged to perform songs from their own background during cultural meetings. This is especially on display in migrant

---

5      Examples of these songs would include, "The wheels on the bus go round and round" (in Danish) and several "good morning" songs. Though references to God in some songs are acceptable, leaders are careful not to reference "Jesus" or anything specific to Christianity, due to the interreligious composition of the group.

church settings, which have been most particularly effective in helping refugees, who have been granted asylum, to establish networks and find identity. Migrant congregations are unmistakably the fastest growing segment of the church in Denmark, and as one might imagine, music usually is "front and center" during worship and other public gatherings.[6] Yet music can also be prominently featured during interreligious refugee events, sometimes with astounding results. A case in point took place in September 2014, when the local Lutheran church in my city of Strandby, Denmark, in cooperation with the Methodist church, co-hosted an event for 200 refugees. The largest groups at the time were from Syria, Eritrea, Somalia, Iraq, and Afghanistan. Before the meeting even took place, some of the hosts were concerned about religious conflicts. The majority of the "guests" were Muslims, and the meeting venue was the *Folkekirke*.[7] Upon arrival, several of the visitors were seen unfurling their prayer rugs in the church's parking lot (as many of us later joked, the church in Denmark needs all the prayer it can get!), while a number of the Christians lit candles in the church's chapel. All concerns quickly dissipated as people greeted each other with smiles, hugs, and displays of gratitude. After the meal, a fellow pastor/musician and I taught the group a few easy to learn "spirituals," after which a member of the Syrian group spontaneously shared a well-known song from his country. The song was downloaded onto his I-phone and we played it over the church's sound system. As the "energetic" song was rhythmically booming out texts the rest of us could not understand, the majority of the refugees present, including many who were not from Syria, began to dance and move freely. The otherwise "subdued" Danish hosts joined in, and one could quickly observe that barriers were dissolved. Muslim women clad in *hijabs* and *burkas* were dancing with Danes, and people from all culture groups were united by a feeling of euphoria and community. The evening continued as representatives from each group chose songs from their national repertoire to share with the entire assembly, with similar results.

It is important to understand that music in itself is not "a universal language." The combination of sound, rhythm, and melody, together with tonal inflections and nuances, instrumentation, and the like is inexorably linked to culture. In other words,

---

6    The Danish organization, KIT (Church's Integration Service) exists to facilitate the migrant church movement and disseminate information. Cf. their website: http://www.kit-danmark.dk/dk/

7    *Folkekirke* is the National church, which is the Lutheran Church in Denmark and throughout most of Scandinavia.

musical expression is just as diverse as linguistics and culture.[8] This means that Danish or Western music in general likely will not have the same emotional impact upon Syrian refugees, for example, as their own indigenous songs. Musicologists understand how scale patterns are arranged differently around the world, which in turn can evoke a variety of emotional responses. Even untrained listeners can "feel" the difference between an Arabic *maqam* and a common pentatonic scale in Western music. Since music appeals to affectivity and the non-rational dimension of human existence, it is exceedingly difficult to pinpoint the processes involved in listening, absorbing, and expressing a piece of music, which in all likelihood was created by a composer who was attempting to convey emotions to the listener. Does the source of feeling lie predominantly with the composer, the listener, the relationship between the two, outside factors, or a combination of these elements? People may differ in their perceptions and understanding of the overall impact of music on emotions (cf. Langer 1951 and Meyer 1968), but it is clear that culture plays a vital part.

On the larger subject of meaning in music, one could argue that it is referential and therefore not universally innate, even though there appears to be some consequences regarding music's impact on the emotions in every cultural context (Meyer 1968:2) The study of musicology across boundaries of culture and ethnicity reveals a common thread in that music, generally speaking, has the intrinsic ability to charge the emotions in ways that little else can (cf. Powell 2016:31-50). That is a key to understanding how even "foreign" music, though maybe less effective in terms of emotional impact, can be a positive tool in building emotional consensus among diverse groups. Susanne Langer contemplated the impact of music on emotions, meaning construction, aesthetics, and the like more than a half century ago, and her words still resonate. In her book, *Philosophy in a New Key*, she explains why music should not be confused with other discursive forms of communication, and quotes:

> "*Music is revealing, where words are obscuring, because it can have not only a content, but a transient play of contents... The assignment of meanings is a shifting, kaleidoscopic play, probably below the threshold of consciousness, certainly outside the pail of discursive*

---

8    As a field of study, ethnomusicology deals directly with the relationship of culture and music.

*thinking… Not communication but insight is the gift of music; in very naïve phrase, a knowledge of 'how feelings go'."* (1951: 243-4)

## Music as Missiological Expression

Awareness of the construction of meaning in relation to music, the impact of culture, and the opportunities created for shared expression provide a segue to deeper metaphysical considerations about the source and impact of music – which brings us closer to the subject of missiology. The nexus between music and missiology is certainly ripe for further exploration. One can indeed ruminate at great length on the therapeutic advantages, as well as the overall affect of music on the emotions. However, from a theological perspective, we assert that music alludes to *transcendence*. Music, in the most ideal sense, can serve as a conduit that connects us to the Creator. A number of scholars have offered deep and thoughtful perspectives on the spiritual dimension of music and the arts, including Jeremy Begbie. In his book, *Voicing Creation's Praise: Towards a Theology of the Arts*, Begbie articulates how artistic expressions are woven into the fabric of the created universe, stating: "Human creativity is supremely about sharing through the Spirit in the creative purpose of the Father as he draws all things to himself through his Son" (1991:179). The historian of religion, Mircea Eliade, notably in his work, *Symbolism, the Sacred, and the Arts*, brought his insights to the subject by presenting an interpretation of reality that understands the symmetry between the sacred and the arts. Among other things, he proposed that art (including music) expresses the fundamental human instinct for transcendence (1986:xi-xii). This is, of course, open to interpretation, and there can be great value in deeply contemplating the connection between meaning construction and music. Yet the idea of transcendence in music, together with the emotional catharsis and connectedness that it offers takes on a particular life in missional contexts, such as refugee work.

The transformative power of music in cross-cultural encounters was cogently expressed in a May 2016 interview with one of Denmark's leading gospel music singers and choir directors, Sofie Hermind. Hermind recounted, among other things, her association with a refugee camp as music therapist. The energy that she described during many of the meetings was palatable. Residents were invited to take part in singing sessions in a "come-as-you-are" environment, and though not all participants demonstrated a particular talent for music, the experience created bonding, broke down barriers, and provided life-affirming impulses to hurting people. Hermind agreed that overtly Christian texts would not have been appropriate, given the constellation of religious backgrounds present at the camps, yet the experience of music in this setting for her was comparable to the ambiance of praise and worship that she regularly has helped to lead in gospel choir gatherings.[9] The spiritual dimension was not lost on Hermind, not least because of the way it included and embraced all people in an atmosphere of love and grace, no matter one's religious or cultural background.

In a number of the gatherings where I have taken part, we have often discussed the extent to which overt Christian texts could be used. During a municipal sponsored culture event entitled, "The Whole World in Frederikshavn" (the name of the city in Northern Denmark where the event took place), the gospel choir from my congregation took on the task of offering a makeshift gospel workshop for any that desired to take part. The songs were chosen carefully, even though we are very accustomed to the phenomenon of even the most secular Danes taking active part in gospel choirs (cf. Lewis 2010). Yet our concerns turned out to be exaggerated as participants expressed delight in singing along, as well as enjoying the opportunity to make new acquaintances. One of the highlights of the event came when the workshop choir led the entire audience in a rendition of "We Shall Overcome." It seems that certain types of Christian music have the ability to legitimate God language in ways that are broadly appealing, for example, African American "Negro" Spirituals and African Gospel songs. This came to light during another occasion, when we were leading a large gathering in the song, "Siyahamba" (We Are Marching in the Light of God). After my music partner and I finished the "set," informal conversations took place with some of the English-speaking refugees in attendance. One man in particular – a Sufi Muslim from Sudan who bore scars of torture and anguish – politely whispered to me: "My brother, I am trying to march in the light of God." Such affirmations confirm that thoughts of God and the meaning of existence are eternally present. The potential for music to communicate God's love and redeeming grace in cross-cultural encounters in ways that are respectful and non-intrusive can remind us that God likewise is present. From a missiological and

---

9    Sofie Hermind is often in demand as a gospel music soloist, in addition to her work as leader of three Danish gospel choirs. Her work at the Sandholm Refugee Camp outside of Copenhagen uniquely qualifies her to contribute to the discourse on music, faith, and interculturalism.

theological perspective, we perhaps can begin to glimpse how the experience of music in such contexts can point to a larger interplay between the human and the divine. That is indeed what seems to be occurring in many of the events that involve meeting grounds where displaced people, multiculturalism, hospitality, spirituality, and music converge.

## LITERATURE

Begbie, Jeremy S.
> 1991    *Voicing Creation's Praise: Towards a Theology of the Arts.* Edinburgh, UK: T & T Press.

Castles, Stephen, Hein De Haas and Mark J. Miller
> 2013    *The Age of Migration: International Population Movements in the Modern World.* New York: Guilford Press.

Dokter, Ditty, ed.
> 1998    *Arts Therapist, Refugees and Migrants Reaching Across Borders.* London and Philadelphia: Jessica Kingsley Publishers.

Eliade, Mircea
> 1986    *Symbolism, the Sacred, and the Arts.* New York: Crossroad Publishing Company.

Langer, Susanne K.
> 1951    *Philosophy in a New Key: A Study in the Symbolism of Reason, Rite, and Art.* New York: New American Library.

Lewis, Mark W.
> 2004    "A Theology of Displacement: Contextualizing the Gospel Among Refugees." Unpublished paper.

> 2010    *The Diffusion of Black Gospel Music in Postmodern Denmark: How Mission and Music are Combining to Affect Christian Renewal.* Lexington, KY: Emeth Press.

Meyer, Leonard B.
> 1968    *Emotion and Meaning in Music.* 8th impression. Chicago, IL: University of Chicago Press.

Moussa, Helene
> 1997    "The Global Culture of Violence and Uprooting," *The Pacific Journal of Theology*, Series II, 18:119-144.

Orth, Jaap and Jack Verburgt
    1998    "One Step Beyond: Music Therapy with Traumatized Refugees in a Psychiatric Clinic." Chapter 4 in *Arts Therapist, Refugees and Migrants Reaching Across Borders*. London and Philadelphia: Jessica Kingsley Publishers. Pp. 80-93.

Petropoulos, Alex
    2016    "Syrian Refugees reveal their Heart through Music." *The Guardian*, February 1, 2016. Accessed April 19, 2016. Available from:
    http://www.theguardian.com/music/musicblog/2016/feb/01/syrian-refugees-reveal-heartache-through-music

Pohl, Christine D. and Ben Donley
    2000    "Responding to Refugees: Christian Reflection on a Global Crisis," in Crossroads Monograph Series, vol. 28. Wynnewood, PA: Crossroads.

Powell, John
    2016    *Why You Love Music: From Mozart to Metallica – The Emotional Power of Beautiful Sounds*. New York, Boston, London: Little, Brown and Company.

Ruud, Evan
    2008    "Music in Therapy: Increasing Possibilities for Action." *Music and Arts in Action*, 1(1):46-60. Accessed April 19, 2016 Available from:
    http://www.musicandartsinaction.net/index.php/maia/article/view/musicintherapy/17.

Scroope, Sarah and Rosemary Signorelli
    2010    "Music Therapy Helps Refugees." *Refugee Transitions*, 23:36-39. Accessed April 19, 2016. Available from: http://www.startts.org.au/resources/refugee-transitions-magazine/issue-23.

# Missiology of Public Life as Resiliency

GEOFF WHITEMAN

DOI: 10.7252/Paper. 000085

Have you ever wondered why some missionaries seem to thrive in the face of unimaginable adversity while others seem to succumb to despair and leave the field prematurely? This question has grabbed hold of me, and lead me to consider everything from assessment to training to care; all critical pieces of the puzzle. In recent years, I've come to believe that resiliency can play an organizing role in assessing, training, and caring for missionaries.[1] Resiliency refers to the process of bouncing back from adversity. As I was contemplating the theme of our conference, Missiology of Public Life, I realized it too could be understood within this construct of resiliency. In this paper, I will: 1) outline a model of missionary resiliency, derived from the literature; 2) reflect on the spiritual and theological implications of this dynamic of resiliency; and 3) offer suggestions of how to apply this model of resiliency to our conference theme, a Missiology of Public Life.

## A MODEL OF MISSIONARY RESILIENCY[2]

Resiliency was first used as an engineering term to refer to "the capability of a strained body to recover its size and shape after deformation caused especially by compressive stress."[3] In a new world made possible by abundant and affordable steel, it's obvious why resiliency would be of interest to the engineers of the railroads and skyscrapers. It should be no surprise that later the term would also pique the interest of psychologists who saw an apt metaphor for psychological resilience as "an individual's ability to properly adapt to stress and adversity."[4]

Emmy Werner was one of the earliest psychologists to study resiliency. In the early 1970's, she began a 40-year longitudinal study with 700 impoverished children from Kauai, Hawaii; these children had been raised in adverse conditions, often amidst poverty and alcoholism. Before her research, it was largely assumed

---

1    See ResilientMissionary.org for current resiliency promoting reflections, services and resources offered to missionaries.

2    The purpose of this section is to layout a basic framework to conceptualize missionary resiliency. Therefore, only a few examples are provided with each section as way of illustration.

3    http://www.merriam-webster.com/dictionary/resilience

4    https://en.wikipedia.org/wiki/Psychological_resilience

that childhood risk factors determined adult outcomes.[5] But she discovered that one third of the children did *not* show destructive behaviors later as adolescents. She labeled this group resilient and thus began the study of how people can respond very differently to adversity. A slew of research has followed in recent decades, especially among children and military personnel.

It should be of no surprise that those concerned with the care of missionaries would also be interested in resiliency. Over the years, a number of articles, books, and conferences have all addressed missionary resiliency. We can compile this collective wisdom into a model of missionary resiliency. The model is simple, composed of three parts: Adversity, Resiliency Promoting Responses, and Possible Outcomes. We'll explore each in turn.

## RECEIVING ADVERSITY

Two of the matriarchs of the missionary care world, Drs. Lois Dodds and Laura Mae Gardner, in their research found that the average level of stress for a missionary was 600% higher than for the average American; this stress hit a climax within the missionaries' first term of service.[6] They believe that the expected stressors of cross-cultural adjustment and external change (which the majority of cross cultural training addresses) were *not* the major cause of attrition, but rather the *unexpected* forces that demand fundamental adaptation to a missionary's core sense of self and worldview.[7]

While there are varying degrees and types of adversity, all adversity by definition reveals the missionary's limits. As Dodds and Gardner's experience confirms, it is impossible to overcome adversity without significantly adapting. Sometimes this means changes in mindset or habit; other times it means shifts in relationships or acquiring new resources. Almost always it involves multiple changes on multiple levels. *This is a critical point: who they are, how they act, and what they have, is not sufficient to overcome the adversity they face—they must adapt.*

5      Worsley, Lyn. *The Resilience Doughnut Model A model showing the interaction of external resources that build individual resilience.*

6      Dodds, Lois & Laura Mae Gardner (2011). *Global Servants Cross-cultural Humanitarian Heroes Volume 2: 12 Factors in Effectiveness and Longevity.* Liverpool, PA; HeartStreams Resources, Inc. pg 143.

7      Ibid pg 145.

In this sense, the most nodal adversities that missionaries face are the unforeseen ones, those unexpected moments that truly test their resolve.

Karen Carr reminds us that pastorally, it's essential to help missionaries accept that the normal responses to adversity, such as depression, anxiety, or post traumatic stress are just that—*normal* responses which are in no way incompatible with resiliency.[8] Furthermore, resiliency must be understood as an ongoing process rather than a fixed quality.

## RESPONDING IN RESILIENCY PROMOTING WAYS

As you might imagine, the type of adversity we are describing impacts the totality of a missionary's life: physically, emotionally, spiritually, relationally—everything. Therefore, a multi-layered response is essential. When we imagine the resilient missionary, David Livingston may come to mind. But this caricature of the rugged lone individual misses the mark. When taken as a whole, the current literature suggests that missionaries respond to adversity in three spheres of their life: *Individual, Relational,* and *Communal.* Research is needed to identify the specific responses that directly correlate with missionary resiliency.[9]

### Resiliency Promoting Individual Responses

First, missionaries can respond to adversity individually in ways that promote resiliency. A foundational response is identifying the meaning associated with the adversity. Knowing that some greater good or purpose may rise from the ashes of adversity makes the experience of and recovery from adversity far more manageable. This is why, as Karen Carr suggests, clearly knowing one's calling is an essential task in building personal resiliency.[10]

Another mindset that promotes resiliency is optimism. Linda Janssen defines optimism in its broader use within Positive Psychology as "active in its

---

8    As I've spoken about my research into resiliency, almost unanimously people respond by acknowledging that they wish they were more resilient. I suspect that the majority people are far more resilient than they give themselves credit for.
9    God willing, research I intend to contribute to through my thesis in 2017.
10   Ibid pg 94.

orientation and focused on the future. It includes finding meaning, setting goals, taking action, conveying gratitude, maintaining perspective, discovering hope and incorporating humor into our lives."[11]

Interestingly, the need for optimism is balanced by the need for lament. Drs. Frauke and Charlie Schaefer, in their development of spiritual resources for resiliency[12] suggest multiple ways to know God's presence and than to respond with lament, forgiveness, and grace. Lament is a process of turning toward God in trust with vulnerable honesty—it is a bringing of our negativity before God rather than directing our negativity toward God. Meaning making, optimism, and lament reframe adversity in a context of hope and represent active, rather than avoidant stances.

### Resiliency Promoting Relational Responses

Second, because adversity reveals personal limits, individual responses are often insufficient. Rather, missionaries need to turn toward their core relationships for support. For many, this often involves their immediate family, host culture friends, and ministry team. Karen Carr suggests that both attitudes and beliefs, as well as knowledge and skills, can be gained through training which promotes this relational resiliency.[13] [14] The attitude and approach of caregivers is extremely important; Carr notes how Job's friends attempt to offer support in the face of his adversity but fail; what is critical for healing in the face of adversity is acceptance and empathy. Such relationships are marked by trust, which needs to be built long before it is needed.[15]

---

11      Janssen, Linda. 2013. *The Emotionally Resilient Expat. Engage, Adapt, and Thrive Across Cultures*. Summertime Publishing. pg. 294

12      Schaefer, Frauke, & Charles Schaefer. 2012. *Trauma & Resilience*. Condo Press. pg. 157-162.

13      Ibid. pg 75-85.

14      One common complexity is that adversity can come from or isolate a missionary from their family and/or ministry team. For this reason, sufficient resources and effort need to be invested into team and family cohesiveness and trust building *before* adversity is faced. Furthermore, missionaries may need resources from outside caring organizations and professionals capable of offering the needed relational support.

15      From my perspective as a marriage and family therapist, I believe that many of the relationship skills necessary for a couple to secure lasting love correspond to the same relationship skills necessary for a successful resiliency promoting relationship among

## Resiliency Promoting Communal Responses

Third, in addition to the immediacy of relational and individual responses, communal responses also play a pivotal role in missionary resiliency. The plans, policies, and procedures, as well as the organizational culture of sending and receiving agencies and bodies, all have direct impact on a missionary's experience of adversity and their capacity to respond. For example, mission organizations can foster cultures that promote wellbeing or foster poor self-care and eventual burnout. They can allocate resources to missionary training and care or expect missionaries to just tough it out on their own.

## REALIZING THE BEST POSSIBLE OUTCOME OF ALTRUISM AND AUTHENTICITY

Adversity leads to various outcomes. Certainly missionaries may be crippled by adversity.[16] Often, they are forever changed by the adversity, and go on to live functional and productive lives. However, it is actually possible to bounce back from adversity *changed for the better*, with the best possible outcome appearing to be altruism. Justine Allain-Chapman in her work in *Resilient Pastors* suggests that adversity actually creates the context for altruism. In other words, altruism isn't possible without first facing adversity.[17] In personal correspondence she shared:

> "From adversity to altruism was my 'original' bit, in my doctorate. People who had had very troubled backgrounds spoke about healing through helping and so I looked at that and saw that there was this process in them and in the biblical material. So often we seem to stop at the encounter with God, when we read

missionaries. See John Gottman. 2001. *The Relationship Cure.*Three Rivers Press for the application of marriage research to other relationships.

16    The unfortunate life of Dorothy Carey comes to mind. See Beck, James. 1992. Dorothy's Devastating Delusions. Christianity Today. http://www.christianitytoday.com/history/issues/issue-36/dorothys-devastating-delusions.html   Allain-Chapman, Justine. 2012. Resilient Pastors. SPCK. pg 30

17    Allain-Chapman, Justine. 2012. *Resilient Pastors*. SPCK. pg 30.

people's stories, but people like Moses encounter and go on to help, or take up pastoral responsibility, and they find their previous circumstances are used by God. It's sanctification and not just salvation, a continuing maturing which involves becoming more whole, I reckon."[18]

Karen Carr develops the work of Yvanne Dolan to refer to this same growth process in terms of three stages: Victim, Surviver, and Celebrant.[19] She describes the celebrant stage as "characterized by fullness, joy and authenticity." It is as if suffering removes the scales from their eyes, and they can now see the suffering of others in a way that compels them to respond. As way of illustration, can you name a missionary saint who did not first face significant adversity? I cannot.

## RESILIENCY AS SKILL AND BUFFER

This paper has proposed a model of understanding missionary resiliency informed by the literature as 1) receiving adversity which reveals a missionary's limits, 2) responding individually, relationally, and communally in ways that promote resiliency, and 3) realizing a best possible outcome of authenticity and altruism.

It's worth noting that resiliency-promoting responses do not represent qualities that are ether present or absent, but rather are skills that can be taught, practiced, and mastered. Furthermore, resiliency functions similarly to exercise: the more you do it, the better you become at it. This means resiliency can help you face a current adversity, which functions as a buffer against future adversity. Consider one of the challenges you're facing in your ministry today. Do you think you could have handled that challenge at the beginning of your ministry? I certainly could not have. I hope that this framework has made clear that promoting resiliency is a more promising paradigm for missionary care than simply reducing attrition.

---

18      email correspondence 5/10/2016.

19      Ibid pg 66-67.

## RESILIENCY AS SACRAMENT AND SANCTIFICATION

This three step framework for resiliency helps illumine Paul's strange words in Romans, that Christians "rejoice" in their suffering. We can endure, but how can we rejoice in suffering? Paul goes on to say, "…knowing that suffering produces endurance, and endurance produces character, and character produces hope, and hope does not disappoint us." (Romans 5:3-5, RSV). What Paul is addressing here is the spiritual implications of resiliency. We could translate this into our model of missionary resiliency and say "suffering produces resiliency and resiliency produces altruism, and altruism produces hope, and hope does not disappoint us." I'd like to develop this to show the sacramental dynamic of resiliency which results in our sanctification through participation in the divine life of the Triune God.

The sacramental dynamic of resiliency is best illustrated through the Eucharist. In the Eucharist we offer bread and wine and receive something entirely different: the body and blood of Christ. However, this dance of receiving and offering extends far beyond the Liturgy. It begins not with our offering to God, but with God's offering to us. God gives to us water, salt, wheat, grapes, and even yeast floating aimlessly through the air. These are symbols of the totality of creation offered to us. We receive these gifts and through our effort turn them into something entirely different—bread and wine which we offer back to God. God receives our offering of bread and wine and again offers something different back to us, the body and blood of Christ—himself. We receive Christ as our very source of life, and as we leave the Liturgy and journey into the world, we too offer ourselves back to God through the living out of our life in the context that we find ourselves.

This Eucharistic dance is allegorical to the resiliency model we just developed. Resiliency begins with the receiving of adversity. Next, the missionary, through their own effort responds to that adversity in ways that promote resiliency individually, relationally, and communally. This response is an offering to God. God receives their offering and offers back to them something entirely different—a capacity for authenticity and altruism which they in turn receive and offer back in a life lived for the sake of others.[20]

Without the eyes of faith, none of us would look at bread and wine and believe, "Divinity is present there," or at adversity and say "The abundant life I really want is there." Yet, both are true, for this is the foolishness of the Gospel—If you want to save your life, you must lose it, if you want to live, you must pick up your cross and follow Christ.

Second, this sacramental dynamic of resiliency also reveals that the best possible outcome, an authentic and altruistic life, is actually an avenue toward sanctification through participation in the divine life of the Triune God.

Jesus' crucifixion and resurrection represent the ultimate act of resiliency. In the Orthodox mindset, Jesus' crucifixion is the conquering of death by *death*. That is to say the joy of Easter Sunday does not nullify the sorrow of Good Friday, rather it reveals that the cross—an instrument of death—is in reality a life-giving cross. Our experience of adversity as essential for resiliency reveal this same reality.

Furthermore, for many missionaries their experience of adversity becomes an appropriation and even participation in the crucifixion and resurrection of Jesus. They come to know Jesus by sharing in his suffering through their suffering. Through the experience of healing prayer, they may realize that not only have they participated in Jesus' suffering, but Jesus has participated in their suffering. He has co-suffered with them. This perichoresis or interpenetration is an encounter with the Incarnate God—Jesus who is Emmanuel. Any theology of resiliency needs to begin here—not solely with the sovereignty of the transcendent God whose ways are not our ways (Isaiah 55:8-9), but first with the empathy of Emmanuel, with the God who "empties himself of all but love"[21] to radically join us in our actual experience.

Through our "deaths" and "resurrections"—our adversity and resiliency, we participate in the very life of Christ. Furthermore, this participation in the life of Christ cannot be divorced from a participation in the mission of Christ which is a participation in the *Missio Dei*. Jesus says in John's Gospel, "Peace be with you.

---

20      Justine Allain-Chapman notes that the church in her wisdom has given us seasons of adversity such as Great Lent which help us to develop our resiliency.

21      Charles Wesley, 1738. *And Can It Be That I Should Gain?* Psalms and Hymns

As the Father has sent me, even so I send you" (John 20:21, RSV). Ultimately we are sent by Christ just as Christ was sent by the Father. That is to say, we too participate in the *Missio Dei*, we too have an active role in the Meta-Narrative of God's redemptive work.

The argument I'm putting forth here, is that our participation in the *Missio Dei* is actualized principally through our offering to God of our adversity and resiliency—a life of successive "crucifixions" and "resurrections." I believe this is the essence of Jesus' command that those who would become his disciples must deny themselves daily, pick up their cross, and follow Him (Luke 9:23). If we stopped here, we would be at risk of a sadistic heresy of asceticism for asceticism's sake. We find a created tension in Jesus' command that the heavy laden should come to him for rest (Matt 11:28) and that he came that we might have life abundantly (John 10:10). Here is perhaps one of the greatest paradoxes of the Christian life; resiliency cannot be separated from adversity for life comes through death.

Therefore, resiliency is not only a helpful paradigm for the practice of missionary care, but it is deeply rooted in the foundational dynamics of the spiritual life—a sacramental participation in the death and resurrection of Jesus, and the *Missio Dei* empowered by the Holy Spirit. In this way, a missionary's vocation is not simply a proclamation of justice and justification to those who are unsaved as those who are saved, but also the actual process by which they themselves are being saved.

## Application to Missiology of Public Life

The theme of our conference is a missiology of public life. As I was reflecting on our theme from the context of my study of missionary resiliency I realized that a missiology of public life is actually an act of resiliency in response to the adversity of globalization. There are countless examples of the dramatic impact of globalization which have impacted every area of our life and every arena of our world. In this sense, we can frame globalization within our model of resiliency as an adversity that reveals our limitations.

How do we respond to the adversity of globalization in ways that promote resiliency? Certainly the desire to forge a missiology of public life is essentially a meaning making task. As such it represents a primary resiliency promoting response. If we think about a missiology of public life within our model of resiliency than we can further identify other individual, relational, and communal responses that will help to shape this missiology of public life. I'd like to suggest three ways that a missiology of public life, seen as a resiliency promoting response to the adversity of globalization, might manifest.

First, a missiology of public life needs to be grounded in optimism in the broadest sense of the term. Our mission is a participation in God's Mission—the God who not only invites us to be co-laborers, but also to become His beloved and to share in his divine life. This is the nexus from which our missiology of public life flows. Second, our missiology of public life needs to lead us to develop a relational response that takes seriously the potential of kingdom partnerships that are marked by oneness rather than sameness. In our globalized context, efforts to partner with others, and especially the "other" will form the networks that are best positioned and equipped to respond to the adversity manifest through globalization—none of us is sufficient alone. Finally, we need a communal response that looks in two directions. First, it needs to be ecumenical, looking around and making space for the diversity of voices which create the choir of Global Christianity. Second, it needs to be orthodox and look back in fidelity with the Universal Church. These two movements, of solidarity and fidelity, are essential if we are to forge a missiology of public life.

## CONCLUSION

This paper has sought to develop a model for missionary resiliency derived from the current literature. This model begins with receiving adversity which reveals a missionary's limits; then responds with resiliency-promoting responses at the individual, relational, and communal level; and finally realizes a best possible outcome of an authentic and altruistic life. Next, I suggested that this model has important spiritual implications as a sacramental participation in the divine life of the Triune God. Finally, I proposed that our missiology of public life is an act of resilience in response to globalization. Furthermore, that such a missiology must maintain an optimism rooted in the *Missio Dei*, be attunes to the capacity of Kingdom Partnerships, and be communal—listening with one ear to the diversity of voices that mark Global Christianity and with the other in fidelity to the Universal Church.

Our model of missionary resiliency ended with a promise of the best possible outcome. I'd like to end this paper with the same for a missiology of public life. I believe that a missiology of public life that responds with robust resiliency to the adversity of globalization may be an offering which God can receive and transform into our best possible outcome. Imagine if this generation might be the church that fulfills Jesus' prayer, "I do not pray for these only, but also for those who believe in me through their word, that they may all be one; even as thou, Father, art in me, and I in thee, that they also may be in us, so that the world may believe that thou hast sent me" (John 17:20-21 RSV).

## WORKS REFERENCED

Allain-Chapman, Justine
    2012    *Resilient Pastors*. SPCK

Beck, James
    1992    Dorothy's Devastating Delusions. Christianity Today. http://www.christianitytoday.com/history/issues/issue-36/dorothys-devastating-delusions.html

Dodds, Lois & Laura Mae Gardner
    2011    *Global Servants Cross-cultural Humanitarian Heroes Volume 2:12 Factors in Effectiveness and Longevity*. Liverpool, PA; HeartStreams Resources, Inc. en.wikipedia.org/wiki/Psychological_resilience

Gottman, John
    2001    *The Relationship Cure*. Three Rivers Press.

Janssen, Linda
    2013    *The Emotionally Resilient Expat. Engage, Adapt, and Thrive Across Cultures*. Summertime Publishing. pg. 294 merriam-webster.com/dictionary/resilience ResilientMissionary.org

Schaefer, Frauke & Charles Schaefer
    (2012)    *Trauma & Resilience*. Conde Press.

Wesley, Charles
    1738   *And Can It Be That I Should Gain?* Psalms and Hymns.

Worsley, Lyn
    N.D.  *The Resilience Doughnut Model A model showing the interaction of external resources that build individual resilience.* http://www.resiliencereport.com/var/file/research/The%2 resilience%20doughnut%20general%20paper.pdf

www.ingramcontent.com/pod-product-compliance
Lightning Source LLC
Chambersburg PA
CBHW070536030426
42337CB00016B/2219